PREACHING AS SHARED STORY

by

LeRoy Kennel

KENDALL/HUNT PUBLISHING COMPANY
Dubuque, Iowa

Copyright ©1987 Kennel Associates

Library of Congress Catalog Card Number: 87–82361

ISBN 0–8403–4528–3

Printed in the United States of America
10 9 8 7 6 5 4 3 2 1

CONTENTS

FOREWORD

I first heard of the possibility of *Preaching As Shared Story* in an elevator in Chicago's Palmer House, where LeRoy Kennel and I were both attending the 1986 Annual Meeting of the Speech Communication Association. LeRoy knew of my professional interest in preaching and story. I am a past-president of the Academy of Homiletics and the current chairperson of the Academy's research group on narrative preaching. I knew of LeRoy Kennel's competence as preacher, teacher and writer. Our association spans two professional organizations and includes collaborative work on *Homiletic,* a journal of which I am the General Editor.

Unlike many of those who write about preaching and story, Kennel states what he means by juxtaposing those two terms. "Preaching," he asserts, "is the art of sharing our narrative history." It is the story of individual human lives structured in larger social and mythic stories. Even more specifically, he declares preaching to be the art of sharing "that drama of salvation which has a narrative quality in which we who were no people . . . are overcoming our identity crises and we who were without purpose now have a mission and ministry, and thus 'the story of our lives.'"

There may be some who will find such a broad definition of "story" disappointing. It does not permit a sharp and relentless focus on the specific questions of biblical exegesis, of doctrinal narration, and of sermonic form which often plague preachers interested in preaching and story. And yet, it is Kennel's breadth of definition which gives this book its peculiar strength. It allows Kennel to tell the story even as he writes about it. And his sense of that story as a living one is never diminished. Kennel's broad definition of story also enables him to outline an informative and helpful "community hermeneutic for sermon research." This hermeneutic includes the interpretation of scripture, the interpretation of history and heritage, and the interpretation of current cultural artifacts.

In emphasizing the breadth of Kennel's definition of "story," I would not want to suggest that the book is devoid of particulars. That is hardly the case. Kennel's experience as preacher and as teacher of preaching issues in innumerable insights, references and examples on a score of subjects. His acquaintance with research being done in a number of fields which investigate human communication adds a dimension often missing in homiletical literature.

I am glad that *Preaching As Shared Story* did not remain simply a possibility. This book provides LeRoy Kennel with a vehicle for organizing and sharing years of lively study and reflection on preaching. This book can provide readers with a view of story and preaching which will expand their understanding and their possibilities for proclamation.

Richard L. Thulin, ThD
Ulrich Professor of the Art of Preaching
Lutheran Theological Seminary
Gettysburg, PA 17325

PREFACE

This is a book about how to prepare and share good sermons. It is both practical and to a certain extent philosophical, since it deals with what a sermon ought to be, where its ideas came from, how they are shaped and organized, and how they can be given their most effective form.

At the heart of this book is the concept of a sermon as a shared story. Such a sermon has seven governing theses:

- It is based upon the story of God's relationship with people.
- It embraces a faith-truth in the Bible.
- It includes a dialogue with a biblical faith-truth taken from a historical event.
- It incorporates a current faith-truth found in the congregation and culture in which the sermon is delivered.
- It is cast in an appropriate style and design.
- It is prepared and presented by convinced preachers and congregational storytellers.
- It is effective with an appropriate worship service.

People want good sermons, but they have lowered their expectation level. This book aims to increase the level of success in preaching and the extent to which sermons exceed expectations. Its intended audience is the preacher in the solitude of his or her study, the student preparing for a life of preaching, and the congregations and parishes in which preaching can become a meaningful and rewarding event shared by both preacher and people.

The kind of sermon described here is one particular story of our lives emerging from the fusion of several distinct vantage points. Its model is the preaching of Jesus, whether to a multitude or to two down-hearted stragglers on the road to Emmaus. It is preaching not restricted to time or place, not fettered by clock or stained-glass window, but free to work its wonders through all the hours and days of those who share in it, wherever they may go.

Indeed, the Bible gives us an instructive example in the story of Jesus appearing to two people on their way to Emmaus after Easter. He confronts them with a simple but existential question: "Why are you so sad?" When they share their hurt, Jesus interprets their history and their lives by interpreting scriptures for them. (The word used in the original text to describe that story-event is *homilein* from which we derive homiletics—the art of teaching preaching!) The hearts of that Emmaus congregation were warmed. Their minds were stimulated, their emotions stirred, their wills moved. They wanted Jesus to stay and preach to them some more.

This is precisely what happens in a shared story sermon, an experiential process of empathy that brings men and women and God's word into harmony.

To bring these considerations into some form of concreteness and specificity, to bring them to hand, the book includes numerous examples of the elements that go into a shared story sermon (that illustrate the "how to apply") and a sort of step-by-step Pilgrim's Progress through the creation of two actual sermons (chapters 2–6) that I've done based upon its principles. However, the study and application of any one chapter can serve as a mini-course in that aspect of the art of preaching.

LeRoy E. Kennel

I. THE STORY IDEA

Thesis 1: A Shared-story Sermon
Is about God's Relationship with People

"God created man because he loves stories," writes Ellie Wiesel. But who, indeed, is the lover of stories—God or Man? Does God love to tell and retell the story of creation in each of our lives? Or is it *we* who love stories, telling them as an act of vocation and a means of exploring our own origin, identity, and relationship with God?[1]

Storytelling, like preaching, is not a solitary pursuit. It involves a storyteller, a listener, and a "something communicated" that binds teller and listener in a relationship that has the power to enlighten us, to change our perceptions, even to redirect our lives. In examining the method and ministry of preaching as shared story, we take our start with the thesis that God's relationship with people stands at the heart of religious communication.

Why do we enjoy and profit from stories and story telling? The answer, in part, is that storytelling allows action and experience to combine in such a way that we can recognize ourselves even as we participate in the story. Participative storytelling goes beyond the mere recreation of reality, the telling of something that happened. In its telling, it creates additional experience. Like a magnet passed over a paper of iron fillings, the act of storytelling can reorient our lives. Where there are formlessness, it can create form and meaning.

A story is a minister of meaning when it possesses the metaphoric and imaginative power to move beyond the story itself. As this occurs, we experience the story as "soul-making", creating a clearing in our lives where "gods play and angels speak". Such stories become visible psyches because they provide visions and alternatives, projections and reflections. Moreover, they become contemporary mythologies, enriched by one's most personal, mundane, and sacred moments. This is why Stephen Crites proclaims that "a religious symbol becomes fully alive to consciousness when sacred story dramatically intersects both an explicit narrative and the course of a man's personal experience."[2]

Models of such storytelling exist. For Albert Lord, a master singer of tales, singing tales was at once transmission of tradition *and* creation of a new and living spirit. Lord insisted that tradition is not "inert acceptance of fossilized corpus of themes and conventions but an organic habit of recreating what has been received and passed on."[3] An epic is not merely past but present, not merely a genre but a way of life.

Frederich Buechner's writings also demonstrate the potential of story methods and motifs for preaching. His *Telling the Truth: The Gospel is Tragedy, Comedy, and Fair Tale* looks to the Bible as a record of the tragedy of human failure, the comedy of being loved overwhelmingly by God despite that failure, and the "fairy tale" of transformation through that love.[4] Buechner un-

1

dergirds these storytelling motifs with experiential bases. The "once-upon-a-time" biblical story becomes a "continual now". The temporal of *then, always,* and *now* converge. Buechner's preaching as story shows the practice of putting these horizontal theses into a vertical one-thus, a literary trinity. The essence of his story is a "fairy tale", that which transcends time. But it is not just any fairy tale. Gospel story is life-story transformed by God's love.

Buechner demonstrates further that the potential of story methods and motifs for preaching is not limited to biblical life-stories; it may begin with, and will likely include, the story of the storyteller. Autobiographical story is both source and resource. His later trilogies of *The Sacred Journey* illustrates how God's words may be unfolded in one's own journey of self-discovery.[5] With commendable artistry, Buechner reflects on key moments of his life from childhood through seminary and finds that God's "incarnate language" indeed can be heard in sounds of nature, children's laughter, the silence of a father's suicide. Whether one's response is intense joy or severe depression, hearty laughter or times devoid of emotion, the author shows the reader that even here is the focus of understanding. Here for instance, is how Buechner uses autobiographical story for creating and communicating relationships:

> The question the neighbors asked him they asked without words and without a word the doctor answered them. . . . What I knew then, without knowing that I knew, was that to see the dust, the fireflies, the green lawn, in their truth and fullness is to see them, as a child does, already clothed with timelessness. . . . They were the Atlases who held the world on their shoulders. . . . The crow of a rooster. Two carpenters at their work in another room. The tick-tock of a clock on the wall. The rumble of your own stomach. My point is that all those sounds together, or others like them, are the sounds of our lives.

The point and power of Buechner's art is to let the story interpret the reader or hearer. Here, Henry J. M. Nouwen says, is "the awesome story of God in the life of an attentive human being." Madeleine L'Engle adds: His story is mine, as mine is his, and it awakened in me 'a sense of the uniqueness and mystery and holiness' of all of us as we search for a self which can be found by God."[6] Like Alfred Lord, Buechner illustrates how a story functions to acieve relationships, not only with one's self and others, but with God.

Indeed, can preaching be anything other than story-telling? Even our lives are stories, and we recognize in the stories of others something of the kind of story we understand our own life to be enacting.[7] Preaching is the story of our lives structured in larger social and mythic stories in which we see both the personal and corporate story taking place. Preaching is the art of sharing our narrative history. It is a present event with a timeless perspective. As with all narrative histories, where there is a sense of the past, there will be anticipation of the future. The preacher story teller will be "about the Father's business" of creating a growing recognition of meaning within the listener's experiences and existence.

The Theology of Preaching as Story

Since preaching is a special form of communication, we are obliged to ask about the purposes of this communication, the "why" or theology of preaching, before we inquire about its process or practical theory.

Preaching as story has at least five characteristic purposes, each of which is explored here and which is elaborated in Appendices.

As an Act of Creation

Whatever else communication is, it is an act of creation. The biblical story reflects the personality of God, whose creativity is itself manifested in the Creation. The scriptures are the story of God creating a caring, celebrating, community and covenant, and of how that community responds. Jesus, in particular, reveals God's creativity as a caring and loving person.

Our response to God's creativity is one of creativity as well, an imaginative and symbolic expression of what becomes rooted in the center of ourselves. Hearing and responding to the old, old story, we re-tell it to ourselves and to others. Our perceptions change, our identity alters, our vision focuses. The result of recreation, renewal, rebirth, reminder. All of these possibilities inherent in the notion of preaching as story are dependent upon God, the chief actor. They also depend upon us as channels of God's word. Whether we produce a double image (contradictory), a fuzzy picture (a snow job), a partial picture (head in the air or feet off the ground) depends a great deal on whether we have been fine-tuned, whether we have received our signals clearly, and whether in the studio of our understanding we can recognize the elements of a real good story.

As an Act of Incarnation

When we communicate, we "take ourselves along": The word made flesh equals the expressed word, of which Jesus is the supreme expression. Communication is most real when reality is incarnated, and most effective when "receivers" can psychologicaly identify with the "sender". We are always communicating something, even what we are.

Preaching as story is about incarnation. Incarnation can be measured in many ways, some of which we will consider later; but certainly one aspect of incarnation is credibility—the way in which we are perceived by others as being safe, competent, and vital. Paul, for example, regarded the community at Corinth as "his letters of recommendation". Incarnation can be evaluated negatively, as the absence or elimination of defensiveness, distortion, manipulation, and symbolic carelessness. These are barriers to communication. Positively, according to the famous quotation of Philip Brooks, incarnation is "truth through personality". And it is recognizable:

One stood in the pulpit,
Face contorted with fervent righteousness hyped up to joy,
And tried to outsmile, outsing everyone.
Each gesture and grimace was practiced, polished and perfectly timed
And seeing him we winced, went hungry.

Another trembled as he spoke,

Striving for self-mastery and failing (almost) utterly,
Yet was possessed beyond himself by caring.
Unaware whether he said ay-men or ah-men,
Nor disturbed by bobbling Word,
He spoke to God, and for and to us,
And seeing through him
(or was it God through him, enabling us to see ourselves?)
We worshipped.[8]

As an Act of Revelation

There are revelations of principles as well as persons. When our personal lives are an incarnation of God's love, like Hosea in his relationship with Gomer, or Paul in his outburst that "nothing can separate us from God's love in Christ," they dramatize a *particular* message. They reveal God as a "friend", a cosmic lover who invites into a relationship and who participates personally. This picture is in sharp contrast to an exemplification of a God who drops fiats or *ex cathedra* pronouncements out of the blue, who attempts to command or force the will. Instead, the incarnation of God's love reveals God as one embracing truth that can be discovered, known and experienced in person-to-person ways rather than as propositional statements which are "delivered".

Preaching as story is an act of revelation. The story ideas emphasizes a retelling of ways in which God has "worked" in a dialog-relation model. Revelation can be viewed as communication about God, provided that communication includes:

1. *word* as retelling of the history of revelatory events;
2. *tradition* as living history which is re-thought and researched for meanings for present existence;
3. *community* as sharing of memory and hope recounted in Old and New Testaments and in church history books;
4. *goal* as increase of love of God and neighbor and oneself, or as attitudes of gratitude and praise of God along with operational goals of discipleship. So viewed, revelation is not something placed in a box as possession; it is not abstraction or concept, proof or argument, principle or preacher. It is a recurring event as we remember the center of our faith and relive it through expression and communication. It is the linking of our internal history with that external history.[9]

As an Act of Interpretation

History and hope are brought together in religious communication. Tevye in *Fiddler on the Roof* illustrates the need for interpretation in his song, "Tradition". One by one, his daughters get married to men of differing backgrounds (and realities). Tevye embodies the dramatic narration of a life—the story out of which emerge identity, worth, and future. He seems not only to agonize but to celebrate the possibility of rising above frustration. This is the precise task of interpretation in religious communication. The biblical story includes the story of the Jews being delivered from Egypt, escaping the problems of the wilderness and passing into the promised land. One counterpart is the story of the Blacks' soul struggle, moving from rural lynchings to mayoral candidates of major cities: theirs, too, is a passage over the Red Sea into a promised land. In light of such possibilities within our religious tradition, unimaginative and uninspired tellings are heresy.

Preaching as story is an act of interpretation. The story of Jesus, the story of Israel, the biblical story can be told in ways that echo and resound in contemporary spirits. "My story," "your story", "our story" are parts of and contribute to the story of people, and the people-story is our story. Reuel L. Howe suggests how preaching can interpret the Christian drama so that it helps people recognize, assemble, and narrate to themselves the meaning of their own life's events and events of their sisters and brothers:

> The Jesus story must become my story and my story must become the Jesus story. I, too, was born, tempted, and trapped between the tensions of legalism and love. . . . Tragically, much Christian teaching has dehumanized Jesus and removed him from us so that he seems alien and separated. I can follow him, not by living his story in me, but by living my story with his. Only then can I tell his story with conviction which then makes it our story. Our story is the story of a pilgrim people living out the drama of human growth and retreat, achievement and failure, sin and forgiveness, trust and fear, death and triumph.[10]

As an Act of Community

Religious communication is a partnership. The very word, "Adam", means everyone and as used in Old Testament thought, as well as by Paul in Romans 5 (in Adam we will die and in Christ the new Adam we are all made alive), the prevailing concept is that of corporate personality. The importance of community is further evident in Jesus' recommended prayer of "Our Father", as well in the word, "koinonia", used 40 times in the New Testament to describe Christian corporate fellowship. When communication becomes communion, privatism is transcended. The vision of the big biblical sermon (Genesis through Revelation) shows God creating a world for community.

Preaching as story is an act of the church. The dialog between God and humankind continues on. Creation continues ceaselessly with and among people. Preaching *is* the church, the community of faith, telling the story of themselves in relationship to God throughout history. A given sermon is a freshly declared and reinterpreted message to persons who live within the instant and changing actuality of history, declares Joseph Sittler in *The Anguish of Preaching.*[11] It is an old story, but it is also ever new. Preaching is not just past messages, "tapes played back", but messages that carry new insight for "today". It is not a solo performance but a corporate function. The whole community of faith is telling the story to themselves and to others. A theology of story is a theology of the community of faith, a contemporary and corporate reincarnation. See Appendices 1 and 2 for additional descriptions of the theology of preaching as story.

The Theory of Preaching as Story

The theology of preaching as story, its purpose, deals with the relationship between God and human. The theory of preaching as story, the process of communication, deals with the way in which humans use symbols.[12] Communication is a gift, a God-send, a grace. This gift includes tools with which to communicate: we have voices, bodies, minds, feelings, and one another.

Communication models show communication as process, something dynamic and not static. In writing about it, we "freeze" the action so that we can look at it more closely. The model reveals: an agent (or source or messenger) sends a message (thought or feeling) through a medium (channel of communication, such as books, music, sculpture, sermon) to a recipient (receiver), who interprets the message and subsequently returns a new message (called feedback). This occurs within a context—a frame around the picture—which tells us where the communicating event is occurring, and the conditions influencing what is sent and what is meant.

The communication process begins with a source who has an idea or a feeling. That "message" can arise from the inner history of the sender or find its source in outer history—the environment, the social context, the accidents and the accents of life—or can be triggered by feedback or a message sent from another source. One's attitudes, information level, ability to communicate, values, role in society all help shape the message and determine how it is sent. These "inputs" for the source apply as well to the ability of the receiver to interpret the message and to generate a response. Source and receiver stand in a one-to-one relationship within the social system and culture. As they communicate they will seek to find areas of common ground or identification. Linguistics points to symbols, common names for common experiences, as bridges to communication. Psychology points to overarching archetypes and myths. Learning theory names common stages of development shared by source and receiver. Because of the dynamic nature of life experiences, and our responses to them, this common ground changes with each engaged act of communication. Participativeness, thus, is a key dynamic in communication.

Story, in particular, invites co-action, plunging deeply into the psyches of participants. Storytelling and storylistening becomes a circular process: the teller visualizing from the right hemisphere of his/her brain and narrating from the left, while the listener hears via the left hemisphere and visualizes with the right. Story participativeness results in part because of visualization and fantasy.[13]

This communication cycle can be interrupted, however. "Noise" is not limited to jet planes overhead; it also results from internal defensiveness, lack of trust, and a resistance to new materials and myths. When we tell others what we think or feel there is no guarantee that we will truly be heard. Defenses also inhibit the listener from responding to a message in authentic ways. Communication may break down because of mispronunciations and misperceptions. Failure may occur because of differing meanings associated with the verbal, visual, and vocal symbols. Despite these barriers, however, the communication cycle can be maintained. Some communication contexts permit immediate paraphrases of what was heard; some permit questions for additional information or feedback; some permit the speaker to try again, shifting one's perception of the common ground between source and receiver. Kenneth Burke's dramatic model in Appendix 3 suggests further ways to achieve "identification" between speaker and audience.

II. THE STORY BOOK

Thesis 2: A Sermon Is Based upon a Faith-trust in the Bible

The story is a mediating form of active consciousness. It's no accident that homiletics and hermeneutics, the respective arts of preaching and interpretation, both derive from the WHAT-LANGUAGE word, "hermes", which means to bring a message from the gods. But what is the message? What is the *story?* What are its roots and how is it nourished from text to sermon? An essential part of preaching as story is laying hands upon the living story.

This double quest we have posited, humanity and God in search of the other, also can be called, "Storytime: God's and Ours."[1] In searching out the nature of this story-drama we can visualize four concentric circles.[2] The innermost circle—let us call it *story idea*—also can be substituted, "the mighty acts of God on our behalf", or, "the personality of the faith". The next circle, *storybook,* gives incarnation to the story. It identifies the story locus, namely, that preaching is rooted in the biblical message. Sermon-stories are not spun from a vacuum, but are located in narrative form of the Old and the New Testaments of the Bible. The third larger circle is that of *story resources,* including past folktellers who lived out and sang out and talked about the storybook-stories around the campfires from 150 A.D. to 1950 A.D. And the final circle is *storyland,* the pastoral, priestly, and prophetic world of the last half of the 20th century.

Advancing from text to sermon requires three exegeses, leading out from the storybook, the past storytellers, and the storyland. Finding a thesis inductively from the scriptures, adding it to one discovered from heritage and history, and then adding to this a thesis from today's world results in a full-orbed "telling it like it is". What is "added up" is not some seriatim, quantitative time-line of three separate exegeses, but one coherent vertical exegesis. It doesn't mater with which stage one starts as long as one encompasses all three, and then returns to the center (the heart of the *story).* For the sake of good relations with the Bible Department, and out of personal bias, we will assume that normally one starts with the scripture. Confessionally, preaching insists on the normative character of the scriptures, viewing them as authoritative for faith and life. And the true tests of authentic preaching has been, and continues to be, whether it is scriptural.

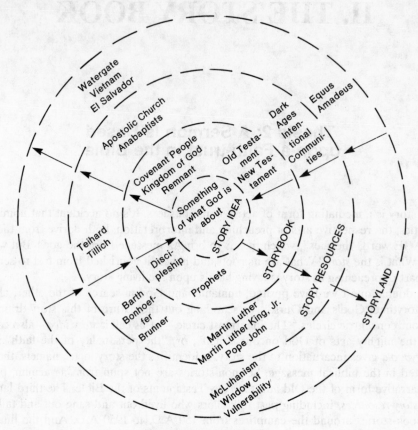

Basic Attitudes

The Bible is a big, diverse, expansive, historical, and oriental book. What attitudes and actions help make up the journey from text to sermon? Five basic understandings for bible study precede five procedures for biblical information.[3]

Attitude 1: Each text is a statement about God and God's self-gifts, with Jesus Christ being the central key and revelation.

Attitude 2: Each text is part of salvation history and has "happened" at a time and place where hard questions had to be answered.

Attitude 3: Each text is fully interpreted when interpreter(s) are reoriented in the process, and when they rediscover how to be faithful people in particular situations and issues.

Attitude 4: Each text is not a private enterprise reserved for scholars and religious experts, but a community venture for discernment and doing of the will of God.

Attitude 5: Each text's authority lies in its bearing witness to the action of God, the activity of the living Lord, the meaning of life within the community of the Spirit for the whole world, and to the event of preaching as storytelling.

Let's illustrate briefly how these five attitudes begin to work on a given subject, such as the "women's issue." When applied attitude 1 appreciates the creation of woman as a good gift: men and women are part and parcel of each other, complementary to one another, true collegues. When applied to passages having to do with the gifts of women, Attitude 2 asks such questions as, To what extent shall the acccent of judgment be placed in our interpretation on the role of women in the fall narrative? How much leadership responsibility did Deborah have? How quiet were the women in Corinth to be during worship? How good was Mary, Jesus' mother, to feel about herself? Attitude 3 states that scriptures about women are not fully intrepreted apart from contemporary considerations, today's particulars—even women's liberation and the struggle for equal rights. Attitude 4 invokes the wisdom of all persons, scholars and servants. it explores the current issues in light of normative biblical data but also in view of the theology of the priesthood of all believers. Women do not quest and question alone. Attitude 5 admits that God is not finished with the subject of the gift of and the gifts of women.

For the fullest exegesis of text, one might read the latest book of sermons by women as well as the most recent article on "Stories of Women in Ministry". This attitude recounts the stories of three Teresas: St. Teresa of Avilla, a prayer warrior, Mother Teresa of Calcutta, the servant warrior, and Sister Teresa of USA, the nonsubservient warrior who didn't kneel before the Pope.

Basic Actions

Joining these basic attitudes in Bible study are five positive and corollary actions. The careful use of these actions in preparing to preach should prevent reading into the text some predetermined answers (the art of eisegesis). Their employment should avoid the detours of false allegorizing, spiritualizing, universalizing, transferencing, and paralleling. Their realization should product normative biblical data for preaching without which we are lost, amnesia victims, not knowing who/whose we are.

Action 1. Determine the original text's meaning by relating to its art form.
   a. Axiom: experience the text as a literary creation, reading it as a letter for the first time, respecting the form that cradles the message, rereading with appreciation for the structure, plot, and plan.
   b. Axiom: experience the literary form/genre, knowing that each kind, exposition, parable, etc., does its own thing, determines what a text offers, i.e., the medium being part of the message.
   c. Axiom: grasp the context, seeing that light comes in light of the full intent of the literary unit.
   d. Axiom: identify that which is special in style, words, phrases, images.

Action 1 helps us to realize that every text has human incarnation, in this case the shape and form of ordinary and generic literature with verbs, nouns, paragraphs, etc. We are invited to be sensitive to the flesh of literary form. As good news, however, the text is already at work to interpret us, shape and reshape, define and redefine.

Action 2. Determine the original text's meaning by relating to the historical situation of the text.

  a. Axiom: trace the ancestry of the text, its variants, sources, original form of tradition, methods of redaction.
  b. Axiom: trace historical and social background affecting form and context, such as the insights of archeology and sociology.
  c. Axiom: identify the author's intent (looking and listening for another or third/author's voice).
  d. Axiom: note how the original audience responded.

Action 2 helps us realize that every text has a historical conditioning, a context, an actual situation which calls out the writing, both in the life of the writer and in the community to which the message is intended. It also shows us the loam from which the text grew—a culture, some prevailing concepts and ideas to which life on the whole conforms itself, a world-view or particular philosophy or theology. Ernest Best encourages us to see that each text is a "freezing of tradition that takes place in a situation, in a culture, through the world-view of the writer on that particular piece"; if any of these elements is present in different amounts, that fact will be reflected in the text.[4]

Action 3. Determine the original text's meaning with the larger biblical story.

  a. Axiom: reflect on the text before going to parallel texts.
  b. Axiom: reflect on the author's intention and theology when compared with texts which have similar themes or issues.
  c. Axiom: permit obscure texts to gain insight from texts which are more plain.
  d. Axiom: appreciate the Bible's overarching consistency, despite multiple theological foci; this allows a given text to be productively correlated with other biblical attitudes, statements, themes, and descriptions.

Action 3 helps us realize that texts may have different meanings and that variant portraits of the same person exist. It is "all right" if there are different "readings" in the Bible because traditions vary. Leander Keck observed that unity doesn't require uniformity and that the variations add rather than subtract.[5]

Action 4. Determine the original text's meaning in relation to another time.

  a. Axiom: find some contribution from heritage and history.
  b. Axiom: find some community check, such as a commentary.
  c. Axiom: find some confession of faith, or denominational treatment.
  d. Axiom: find some incident in culture that serves as a case study to illustrate the text's thrust.

This action seeks additional "light on the subject" and helps us ascertain whether our own interpretation is on track. As one assumes that the Spirit of God leads in a particular interpretation, so one grants the same dynamic is possible at another time, place, and situation. This action affirms not only that an interplay of interpretations is possible between one text and another, but between the history of the church and every text, and between the world today and every text. Action 4 calls upon the interpreter to use the Christian community for completing insights, for correlating biases of culture, and for curbing whatever ideological accretions may be at work in one's approach to the scriptures.

Action 5. Determine the text's meaning in relation to "this" time (an action of special importance since our goal is to translate the text's meaning into contemporary understandings).

   a. Axiom: paraphrase the scripture with today's language.
   b. Axiom: consider the text in light of the pastoral issues of one's congregation.
   c. Axiom: set the text against the prophetic issues of one's time.
   d. Axiom: invite the text to ask a reponse from us to the God who confronts us in the issues raised by this text.

Action 5 helps us move into the last concentric circle of storyland. It is an action that is as specific as to ask, What problems and potentialities does the text draw out of world, work, play, school, even church? This action fuses the reality of the text with one's own dwelling. It helps a sermon to be priestly, to ask what it means to have "Just a Closer Walk with God", what experience of forgiveness is needed and what area for strengthening is important. It helps a sermon to be pastoral, to show the members of the congregation how to tackle and solve some important problem, some puzzle of mind, or how to ease the burden of conscience or distraction. It helps a sermon to be prophetic, to offer new and, if necessary, confrontive perspectives on our perceptions. It helps a sermon to be pedagogical, to achieve what Anselm saw that faith sought — understanding.

Let's take up the "women's issue" again, by way of example, and see how these five basic procedures begin to work when applied to a given subject. The point here is to illustrate briefly the hermeneutical principles for applying texts in preaching, not to elucidate the women's issue. Action 1's concern for meaning in relation to the passage's art form asks that Ephesians 5:22–24 ("wives be subject to your husbands"), for instance, be interpreted only when the prior verse is considered also, that there be mutual husband-wife subjection. Action 1 demands equal consideration with the succeeding paragraph, vs. 25–30, which qualifies subjection to sacrificial love of the husband and the unity of the marriage partners. Similarly, this action sees Paul's summary of public worship in 1 Corinthians 14:34–35 not only with the thrust of "silence" but with the primary meaning of worshipping decently and orderly (1 Corinthians 14:36–40). The final axiom respescts rabbinic methods of argument common in Paul's days and as employed in 1 Timothy as a "letter" on particular issues at Corinth and Ephesus.

Action 2 stresses the historical situation. It asks, What does "head" mean, not for us, but for Paul? It answers that Paul affirms custom and law, that man is the head of woman, that woman is under the authority of man, as Jesus is subordinate to God. Paul honors distinct male and female roles in worship with male headship. The historical and social backgrounds help determine the meaning since the wearing of "the head covering" is an appropriate cultural expression of subordination in that culture (and expresses here the authority of man). Historical glasses reveal also that language carries a potential sex bias that requires checking if masculine nouns and pronouns are substituted for nouns and pronouns of common gender in the original language. Another related problem is that some version of Romans 16:1 label Phoebe a servant, but elsewhere the word "diakonos" is translated "minister".

Action 3 concerns itself with the larger biblical story. If Genesis 2:23–24, 1 Timothy 2:13, and 1 Corinthians 11:8–9 cast women as to appear inferior and subordinate, Genesis 1's story of creation along with the Gospel's view of women in worship and witness need to be correlated. Genesis 1:26–27 has male and female as harmonious sexes with differentiation that means equality not hierarchy. The gospels written after Paul's letters to not suggest that woman is to be subordinate to man. Scriptures, Romans 13:14 and Ephesians 4:13, teach that the goal of our understanding is not some status-quo stereotype but equality in Christ, and putting on Christ, with new possibilities for each and all. When Action 3, the invoking of the larger biblical story for scriptural understanding, is applied, the utilization of particular scriptures and cultural patterns defer to and even defend the larger goals of the gospel, namely, the orderly conduct of worship, the edification of the whole body, and the primacy of love in human relationships.[6]

Letting other scriptures have their say in arriving at a biblical consensus on whether or not to use male imagery for God is needed also. Is God to be thought of as male? Is the church as a body of Christ something of gender, and if so, female? The verdict is clear if we read other scriptures in faith for faith: Jesus interacted with women; other scriptures analogize God as a mother and a woman.

Action 4 calls for progressive understanding, the adding of knowledge to knowledge, continual testing of the thinking of the "brethren". When the women's issue is applied, this action offers data for both the hierarchical and liberationist interpreters. Using the "incremental" approach, the latter group might label Paul's concern for equality in Christ as moving backward when considering Augustine's argument for female subordination based on the grounds that woman is the weaker vessel, or when noting later centuries' subjugation of women in the church.

Action 4 checks, commenators and scriptural interpreters, do differ, however, as Willard Swartley's case study in biblical interpretation on women reveals. Interpreters themselves are shaped by a complex mixture of psychological, sociological, economic, political, sexual, and religious factors, a blend of influences creating culture and personality which, in turn, serve as a pair of glasses affecting the task of interpretation. The call is to read scripture, as well as the historical treatments, in ways that see something besides one's own thoughts, lest that text becomes a mirror reflecting back only what one wanted it to say. Swartley sides with the liberationists who tend to admit tension, even welcoming diversity of thought on the basis that the biblical view of God is one who encounters the particular "stuff of history and human experience". This historical hermeneutic judges biblical thought as rooted in a "historical community's ongoing relationship with God". This view can be called "the missionary principle of the Bible" which identifies and interrelates both contingent and coherent elements.[7]

Action 5 calls for contemporary perceptions. It asks, for instance, whether the individualism inherent in the 20th century women's movement contradicts the mutual interdependence of *all* created people and *all* recreated by God. Contrarily, this action does not hesitate to confess that this is no longer "a man's world". It recognizes that a new consciousness of women's rights for engaging in gift-giving and receiving is not only possible but promised. It welcomes, not shuns, current debates—even on Scriptural interpretations.

Dynamic Principles

Heremeneutics, James Sanders reminds, can refer either to what one does when reading and interpreting a historical text, *or* how one translates a thought or event from one cultural context to another. Sanders is concerned that both tasks be done.[8] The first task involves principles, rules, and techniques for understanding a text in its original context. The second sometimes engenders tension between Bible and Ministry departments in seminaries.

Three dynamic hermeneutic principles are needed for "scoring" the same point that the original author or speaker intended. The first calls for dynamic analogy, achieved by seeking to identify persons and figures in scripture who may represent different folk today. This requires reading the text in ways that help one to identify with the people in it. One deliberately takes the point of view of the Pharisee, or the person left by the road, or — with enough imagination — even with the stones that would cry out on Palm Sunday. These multiple perceptions open the reader to more of God's message and to God's agenda, rather than merely to one's own.

The second dynamic principle involves telling the story "again" against the backdrop of the continuing saga. Anamnesis (living memory) articulates the tradition and identifies with the faith ancestors, the spiritual uncles and aunts, grandpas and grandmas, and the various "minutes of the past meetings." Being mindful of what God is about in that list of "begats" of Matthew 1, one discovers that God works with many imperfect and inadequate persons. Incarnation keeps occurring: God continues taking on our humanity, fraility, limitations, and weaving them into purposefulness. Proper hermeneutic sequence is discovering what the text shows of God working in and through the human condition before asking what we might do with the human situation in which we find ourselves. "We have first to look for God's work in the stories and then look for ours in the light of his."[9] The Bible is to be read with honesty, humility, and humor — taking God more seriously and ourselves less so.

The third dynamic principles for translating from text into another context involves understanding the Bible as the church's book as a paradigm. This principle looks for the pattern of the function of nouns and verbs in the biblical cultures and appreciates the idioms and metaphors of the various believing communities:

> A paradigm, first, of the verbs and nouns of God's activities and speech, and then, thereupon, a putative paradigm of the verbs and nouns of our activities and speech, in our time and our contexts. . . . The ontology of the Bible as canon is that of paradigm addressing the faithful in context when they seriously ask the questions, who are we and what are we to do? The answers come in paradigms of faith (identity) and of obedience (lifestyle) appropriate to the contexts in which the questions seek them.[10]

Metaphorical Processes

Our discussion of biblical hermeneutics on the interrelationship of revelation and faith, of going from text to sermon, of relating presuppositions and procedures, can benefit from the thinking of semiotics in general, and of the study of metaphor in particular. These disciplines ask that each genre in scripture be examined from the perspective of its literary form to see what part of revelation it contains. (1) The symbol is not just that of translation but also of a myth which opens up a field of experience. The symbol has a double intentionality: one that is literal, and the other with new possibilities to be explored, particularly for relating faith and hope. (2) The response of the "audience" is important: the sense is the message conveyed by "discourse" and the reference is the extralinguistic reality to which it points. One brings faith to a biblical text but also one entertains in the imagination what it would be like to "dwell in the world". (3) Accordingly, we are to be excited not about going back to the situation "behind" the texts but about their reference, what world they disclose "in front of" them. The stance according to one theorist is not of looking in some rear-view mirror but of riding on the car's hood and looking forward.

The study of metaphor calls also for the preparation of oneself for receiving the text's testimony. (1) We do not have immediate self-consciousness but our response is *mediated* by ideas, actions, works, etc., which objectify it. (2) We *belong* to a cultural story; we are part of a tradition. (3) We understand ourselves before the text by *appropriating* what it can teach us about our efforts to exist. We expose ourselves to receive from the text a larger self. We do not submit our wills to the text of scripture so much as we permit our imaginations to be opened to new possibilities. We act our faith as we appropriate the new possibilities.

These approaches to metaphors help to examine parables. Parables convey a certain "sense" and also "refer" to a world. The text stands between its historical-critical anslysis of its backgrounds and the interpretation of its message as kerygma. This process, according to Paul Ricoeur, requires a dialog with structuralism: a symbol's meaning deriving from participation in discourse where sentences, not single words, carry the metaphorical function. Metaphors re-describe reality just as a painting re-describes what the photograph shows or what the eye sees. The parable is a metaphorical process in narrative form "turning on the clash" of these several meanings of the words and surprising us with the new. One metaphor serves as the "root" which gathers others and creates possibilities for endless reinterpretations. The true nature of the "reference" comes when the intersignifications are considered. The text has interpretation possibilities for one's actual social world because of the "believer's" participation.[11] The result of "polyvalent meaning" is not to be construed with the old form of allegorization which disrespected the historical context. It does stand in tension with Jeremias who insisted that we look for the one main point only in every parable. It affirms the creativity which can actually make scripture a spiritual resource.

Imaginative Practices

Religious imagination is yet another way of describing our interactions with scripture. Religious imagination is the creative activity which occurs as a preacher works on a biblical sermon. Creative imagination in action makes us act similar to, and perhaps most like, God. Although "I create, therefore I am" is something shared with all artists, it is something special for preachers. Imagination is life-giving, but religious imagination proceeds from a mystic center and is channeled through biblical revelation:

> The minister consciously studies and ponders that biblical tradition, and expresses insight of language and thought that has continuity with the ancient story. That tradition and the God behind it are the source of light. Scripture becomes a 'glass of vision'. The act of seeing and expressing carries the power of life.[12]

Scripture or "the story book" becomes a glass of vision when processed with the preacher's imagination. Telling the scripture story has power. And such telling gives continuity with the past as well as fresh insight. A teller has "power" if the story is shared by those who hear. When Elie Wiesel repeats an old Chasidic tale of the Baal Schem Toy of miracles happening, because of a repeated story, the communication power is still there in spite of the facts that the "fire" and "prayers" are not. Similarly, "Do this in remembrance of me" has power when Christians celebrate the story.

Mere magic does not produce imagination, however, nor does mere telling the story produce results. "A conscious tie to the divine source" and "a conscious contact with the Living God" must accompany repeated visits to the story book. An attitude of openness seeks for the gift of God. It actively looks for answers to questions such as, "What must we do to be saved?" or "What does the Lord require of me?"[13]

Careful observation and considerable visualization are the requirements for probing life through the power of imagination: "The words of Amos . . . which he saw" (or Isaiah 2:13, Micah 1:1). Amos, while walking down the street, sees someone with over-ripe fruit; he gets a message of an end-time that has come. He observes also a carpenter with a plumb line (and possibly a crooked wall); Amos' imagination produces the thoughts of the nation as the wall and the righteousness of God as the plumb live. What would Amos see today? Would it be that the building up of many more nuclear warheads and missiles to keep American strong is a crooked program that doesn't have any right angles when measured against Jesus' reconciling truth, let alone the plumb line of interdependent trust inherent in the United Nations Charter?

Imaginative connections within, and with, the New Testament are also evident. Jesus gives his inaugural address by quoting from Isaiah and announces that it is fulfilled: that lame will walk, people see . . . the year is acceptable. What follows in Jesus' words and life are not literal repeats but imaginative connections. What happens is not point-by-point matchings; that would be reruns, wooden orthodoxy. Fresh statements occur, states Young, because "Seers are their own persons. They touch base with tradition so as to score on their own . . . always in a posture of setting out not knowing where they are going, yet confident that the journey has some divine underpinnings."[14]

Confidence is the critical factor for imaginative study of scripture. Confidence results when one is delivered from the bondage of "having nothing to say" and the fear of "having no tools" with which to open the story book to others. Possessing the five attitudes plus the five actions, employing Ricoeur's stance of riding on the front bumper looking for the "next signification", and activating Young's "imagination" and Sanders "dynamic principles", there should be "confidence aplenty" to risk going out into a new country of discovery—relying on the Spirit of God.

With the best of attitudes and actions of Bible study, one still may get into hermeneutical or homiletical trouble. One may ask the strongest scriptural questions (What is being talked about—the noun, the subject? What is beind said about it—the verb, the action of the subject?) One may ask the best functional questions (What does it mean for me? What does it mean if lived out and practiced?). And one may still be out in "left field". The safety net is not in any *one* of the approaches alone, but in their use *together*.

A recommended "case study" for applying these attitudes and actions of the Bible study is "Gomer's Side of the Story" prepared by Caroline K. Jonah and Wayen E. Barr, distributed by the Intercollegiate Case Clearing House, Soldiers Field, Boston, MA 02163.

But the research for the sermon-story is not finished. An exegesis of scripture coalesced with an exegesis of history-heritage along with an exegesis of contemporary existence brings the needed coalesced vertical exegesis. This interpretive approach cuts through given stories and produces a new story, congruent with the stories of all time.

Application

In the remainder of this chapter, and in succeeding chapters, two quite different sermons will be developed in stages to illustrate the application of concepts as they are developed. This process will begin with the researching of scriptures and continue through the actual sermon form in Chapter VII.

Sermon 1, the theme of vocational calling

    Action 1: Jeremiah 1:4–10

- Jeremiah is (1) summoned, (2) appointed, (3) known, (4) consecrated.
- The genre is that of a dialogue, a recurring formula for prophets.
- The authenticating of Jeremiah's prophetic ministry was dictated from a backward look. It follows "the title page" of when he ministered, and is followed by two message-images, the almond tree and the melting pot.
- "Calling" is the central image, both his calling from God and his being a "mouthpiece" for Yahweh. Both emphasize a divine encounter, self-discovery and self-surrender, or being chosen and of choosing.

    Action 1: Luke 4:16–20

- The paragraph consists of (1) a reading of Isaiah 61:1–2, (2) its interpretation, and (3) the "congregation's" awareness that something special is going on.
- It is a normal synagogue event of scripture reading and explanation by someone with credibility.
- The preceding paragraph tells us that the home town boy now famous in the surrounding country has come home. His previous temptation of inner decision is now put to test at home.
- Jesus links the "coming age" to himself: the hearing is *now* fulfilled. The congregational response of their favorite son is of both surprise and of skepticism: "Is this not Joseph's son?"

    Action 1: Romans 9:20–26

- An imaginary dialogue of (1) whether God makes one ceramic piece for one purpose and another for a still different reason, and (2) whether such designations of meniality and grandeur is fair.
- The genre is that of an analogous argument.
- This discussion follows a careful cataloguing of how God has been at work in history creating a salvation history with Abraham and the Jewish people.
- Paul's claim that God has had a process of election/selection but reassigning the functions of the differing peoples (pots) almost crumbles when one considers that although people are made of clay they are more than clay. Although probably sensitive to this, Paul insists that God's new relegations (callings) work out for the Gentile advantage.

    Action 2: Jeremiah 1:4–10

Jeremiah looks back to the time of his youthful calling. He can see the "hand" of God in the unfolding events and experiences of his history. His experience parallels with Isaiah's call. Although aware of other prophetic callings, he senses that his is more "global" both with other countries and in tearing down and building up.

    Action 2: Luke 4:16–20

The synagogue's expectations included that of the coming Messianic Age when they would be released from oppression and brokenness. Their response to Jesus' claim to be "leader", however, is met with ambivalence.

    Action 2: Romans 9:20–26

Paul is asking, are the Gentiles now called to be Israel? Has God been creating a situation to bring good out of it, or is God just using a situation to bring good out of it? Paul is clearly saying that God is at work in everything.

Action 3: Jeremiah 1:4–10; Luke 4:16–20; Romans 9:20–26

When these three paragraphs dialogue one with the other, it is clear that they pulsate with a divine and human encounter, an awareness of such Presence in a historical situation, and in particular of a mission to be performed. For Jeremiah it is to tear down and build up not only with the Jews but also with other nations; for Jesus it is to bring in the Messianic Age in which sight comes to the blind, release to the captives, etc.; for Paul it is the respective new assignments for menial and multiple purposes.

When compared with additional scriptures, a pattern emerges. Two uses of *kaleo* occur: the noun and the verb, naming and summoning. Both have their nonliteral usage, however, the psychological-spiritual meanings: (1) claiming by naming, and (2) a serving by summoning.

The metaphorical and imaginative look-forward considerations of Ricoeur, Sanders, and Young call forth the image of the telephone call as a channel of experience through a mouthpiece, both presence and purpose, identification and commission. It, too, is characterized by reason and intuitive recognition.

Sermon 2, the theme of Christ, the water of life

Action 1: John 4:7ff

- Jesus is at Jacob's well in Sychar, Samaria, with three significant conversations: (1) the Samaritan woman and a series of appeals to her, to her sympathy, her curiosity, her conscious need, her conscience, to her religious instincts, to hope, to faith; (2) the disciples, and the arrousal of their amazement and an invitation to them to share in the purposes of his service; (3) the "Samaritan family" with their response of faith and invitation to him to say on.
- The genre is primarily that of interview and conversations.
- The movement of the larger unit is of Jesus going to those who are "outside" including Nicodemus, a Samaritan woman, and then a Gentile nobleman. John's motif seems to be that of "showing" a universal Christ.
- The key word is that of "living water". It is a continuation of the referent of Jeremiah 2:13 where God is viewed as the fountain of Israel. A further figure that emerges is Jacob's well and whether that was the area for "true" worship or at Jerusalem.

Action 2

- The Evangelist John undoubtedly shapes the text to fit his literary purpose of the universality of the gospel, which does not mean that we do not have new material regarding Jesus' desire to get away from the pharisees at Jerusalem and get on with his mission to Galilee, with the intention of going through Samaria to get there.
- The Samaritans were ostracized by the Jews of Judea because they were of mixed blood. With the Pentateuch as their sacred book and offering sacrifices on Mount Gerizim, their sacred place, they, too, regarded themselves as true believers of Yahweh. Since the fourth-century schism the mixed-blooded Jews and the full-blooded Jews were in strained relationships.
- John in his subsequent thought referred to the Holy Spirit as bringing the water of life. John allows us to hear an authoritative "voice" saying that, indeed, this Jesus is God's Son, the true prophet and messiah. John's recorded dialog lets us "in on" Jesus as the true revealer of God, the good news for the whole world, wherein there is a progressive realization that Christ's words and witness fulfills all religions.

- Everyone, it seems, marvels and believes. The Samaritan woman, the disciples, and the anonymous woman's extended family—all, come to belief.

Action 3

Christ is the living water that is offered freely—by grace—to all people. Christ's mission is to all people. All people have their true center in him, not in their traditions, holy places, racial or national loyalties. Jesus is a living fountain and not a stagnant cistern, one who offers satisfaction and life. The new age has come. Not only does Jeremiah 2:13 get addressed, but also such scriptures as Jeremiah 17:13; Genesis 26:19; Psalm 42:1; Isaiah 43:20, 44:3, 55:1; Ezekial 47:1; Zechariah 14:8; Revelations 21:6, 22:1, 22:17.

III. THE STORY RESOURCES

Thesis 3: A Sermon Is Based upon a Dialog of a Biblical Faith-truth With at Least One Additional Faith-truth from a Historical Context

Scripture serves as the sermon's source. Theology, church history, ethics, and culture serve as resources. The distinction does not mean that emphasis on scripture as source ignores religious thought and experience; quite the contrary. One stage of sermon research, as we have just seen, involves examining materials which record the way in which people have lived out their faith. These insights enhance, rather than replace, scripture.

Story resources provide an additional experiencing of the biblical text, retelling and enlarging one's biblical thesis. They are vantage points where revelation and interpretation occur. To call upon them is to recognize that God not only spoke once upon a time but that God speaks whenever scripture is the foundational story, and that God continues to address situations and people.

These resources are both past storytellers and part of the ongoing story. A legal analogy would claim that these additional data are part of the original story: the proceedings of actual "trials" become part of the working material for later cases. These precedents become part of the "working constitution."

Creeds

The most famous of creeds if the Apostles Creed, so named because it contains what the apostles witnessed about Jesus. And now it, too, witnesses. As a witness it is a cornerstone of church thought. Although the precise form of the creed as we now have it did not take shape until the Eighth Century, it was already called an "apostles creed" in 390 A.D. Rufinus wrote a commentary on it in 400 A.D.[1] Incorrectly, he believed that all the apostles met and agreed upon it. Nevertheless, the Apostles Creed has validity for us today—and vitality—because it (1) speaks of the faith of the early church, (2) is a result of Matthew 28:19's great commission to disciple all peoples, and (3) is similar to the baptismal creed used at Rome in which applicants were instructed.

It is probably true, as Andrew Blackwood once observed, that this creed is used more often in public worship than any other form of "sound words." It is located variously in the service, sometimes after a hymn or a reading of scripture, and thus serves as a people's response to God's revelation. It is sometimes placed just before the sermon. Some worshippers stand for its recitation. It is often used as the basis for a series of sermons. Its validity as an ongoing teaching instrument stems from its objective declaration about the trinity of God, its key beliefs of truth and its clear affirmation of the personal faith of early Christians.

Creeds such as this have a rationale. They help define faith. They provide a norm, a standard, a touchstone. They provide material for teaching and preaching.[2] We can seek to find elements in the life and teaching of Jesus, for instance, that throw light upon the words in the creed, and ask, in turn, what the words of the creed tell us about Jesus. There are limitations with creeds, however. Created to meet some particular need or situation, creeds are not complete or final. They express the language and categories of thought of a given time. Without understanding the experience that gave them birth, creeds can become separated from their original function. They may be overly stressed and take upon themselves the nuance of "god".

Confessions

Redactors, the earliest biblical editors, give us some of the first confessions of faith. The study of ways in which written sources and oral traditions were used in writing the scriptures is called redaction criticism. These early "confessors" made faith statements even in their contractions, expansions, omissions, substitutions, ways of connecting pieces of material, interjected comments, and alterations of fact or theological meaning. Redaction affirms biblical truth rather than denies it. Increments and changes in the confessional aspects of faith are part of the ongoing testimony of religious experience.

Most denominations have one or more confessions of faith. Many are rewritten from time to time. With new awareness and integration of experience, confessions need restating. Thus comes refinement. Larger comprehensions cause "new editions". World conditions, scientific discoveries (even nuclear missiles), civil rights, liberation thought—all of these aspects of experience—bring new issues into the open. Several decades ago, the "social gospel movement" resulted in churches seeking to understand and minister to the problems of labor and agriculture. Confessions of faith, resolutions and documents—and the circumstances out of which they came—should be reflected in controversial preaching.[3] They provide relevant message material, a vital resource for preaching, and add to the credibility of the preacher's knowledge.

Characters

When humankind needed a clearer picture of what God thinks, it received one in a person named Jesus. Sermons, too, need to provide vivid pictures; they call for people who hurt, laugh, say "No" or "Yes". Biography is one source of such story material, giving us an opportunity to look at significant persons with the purpose of identifying the beliefs that account for the kind of life they lived. For example, studies of Dag Hammarskjold, Martin Luther King, Jr., Clarence Jordan, and Charles Ives demonstrate that narrative theology can be learned through the story form of biography.[4]

The purpose of investigating another person's story is to learn more about one's self. The investigated character provides a meeting place, a common ground for preacher and congregation. As we return from the lives we have examined, "the examiners become the examined, and our claim on our saints becomes their many-sided claims upon us."[5] The writer of *Hebrews* believes that people-stories are instructive. Having us look at a large gallery of the faithful, we are then admonished to run our race well, laying aside that which holds us back. We are not to worship the saints but let them by their encouragement aid us in our worship. The point: the faith of mothers and fathers lives! These "athletes" who have gone before help train and make ready those who come later. Such biographical investigation has potential problems. We may be tempted to overly admire the saints or to gloss over part of the story. Storytellers who refuse to show the "warts" are refusing to tell the whole story. Seeing the saints in their blemishes and weakness, we know better what is possible for us, even in their strengths and achievements.[6]

Autobiography is a similar resource. Whether it be Augustine's *Confessions* or one's own diaries, this genre has the force to determine how self-deception occurs, for example. We can discover through autobiography that which is latent in our own consciousness.

> Our basic stories and images determine what we discover. . . . Autobiography is the literary form that mirrors the moral necessity to free ourselves from the hold of our illusions through truer images and stories. . . . Christians claim that the truth provides the skills to confess the sin that we do is to be found in the history of Jesus Christ.[7]

Carols

Songs are useful — and beautiful — resources for religious communication. Lyrics can supply ideas and feelings; melodic lines and the harmony or lack thereof, more abstract than words, nevertheless serve as emotional vehicles for religious experiences. A particular genre of music, such as jazz, the spiritual, even rock music, can be examined for its revelation of a mood, a people's pilgrimage, or for its impact upon a participant.

Unfortunately, many hymns are mediocre poetry. They usually reflect a specific or limited time period, without a bridge to our own times. In addition, some hymn writers dwell on tangential aspects of faith as if they were all important, such as the *privatism* of "We walk in the Gardens alone, while the dew is still on . . . " in contrast to the *personal* dimension of "Walk that Lonesome Valley . . . by yourself, no one else can do it for you."

Poetry and myth, whether carols or hymns, words or music, should be examined for multiple meanings, as well as treasured participative encounters. Poetry's value is as a faith statement, not as a scientific document, Platonic abstraction, or example of Aristotelian causation. Poetry is associated with metaphor, the heart of religious language. Experiential and imaginative language is often analogical. Along with myth and story, carols function in a catalytic way in recreating and renewing experience.[8]

Crises

A crisis is not so much a catastrophe as a turning point; in retrospect, when it can be seen clearly and judged fairly, it can provide a story resource worth exploring. Individuals, groups, and institutions all have turning points. Frequently, the critical incidents of one person intertwine with others. Church history is filled with such intersections and critical incidents. Exploration of this resource could include such questions as:

What events have had the most impact upon you?

What interpretation do you put upon these events?

What do you see as the key turning point in history and how do these affect who you are today?

When is the anniversary of your congregation? What important decisions went into its formation? Were there times when people were ready to call it quits?

What led to the Protestant Reformation? How has this affected you?

What caused the formation of a given church creed, council, confession?

The purpose of such exploration is to reflect theologically on history. Where is it moving? Where is God calling people to help it move? Where have people in the past wanted it to move? What can we learn from them? Was the Protestant Reformation a "tragic necessity" due to lack of preaching? Does the post-reformation reveal that Protestants overplayed preaching to the neglect of the eucharist, or of the visual arts? Even recent events are relevant for examining the ways in which theology touches history at a point of crisis. What can be learned from the experience of Dietrich Bonhoeffer's witness against the Third Reich? From the fate of the three Roman Catholic nuns murdered in El Salvador?

Our earlier concern with "characters" as a story resource can be joined with this one. One way of researching religious experience is to look at the anxiety of moving from one stage of life-development to another.[9] Whether our fascination is Erickson's life stages study of Gandhi, Luther, or Jefferson, or Piaget's cognitive development, or Kohlberg's moral stages, or Fowler's faith development, or Westerhoff's faith styles, this approach appreciates the nexus of conflict in human experience. Crises are doors for insight. Thus, writes Regis Duffey, "Experience is at least the narratives of our shared story with our attempts and failures, decisions and indecisiveness, insights and blindness, commitments and irresponsibilities."[10] Crisis, the unsettling event, can be the decisive moment or turning point.

Cases

To take up a case in point is to be specific, for example, with some phase or page of church history. As a resource category, it is not separate from those we have already considered, but it merits special mention because it is an effective method of sermon research. There is also a growing body of literature for story resourcing that uses the methodology of case history.[11]

But case studies are found "everywhere." Almost any theological discussion will have complex ethical implications, personality problems, social involvements—all of these can be elements of the case study. The biblical case study referred to in the previous chapter on Gomer in the book of Hosea is but one level of study. There's a larger choice: Will the professor of Old Testament compromise himself and introduce the book of Hosea in the chapel service for the student preacher, when it might give tacit approval of an inaccurate exegesis and incorrect thesis? This is the genius of the case study: it provides a way of examining the choice of different paths, the resolution of conflict, the understanding of self-deception, the paths in which the Holy Spirit can "lead."[12] Theologians and ethicists, such as Stanley Hauerwas and James Wm. McClendon, Jr., are now saying this is one way to understand our faith and make our decisions. McClendon's conviction is that any given story is inadequate, taken alone: it is "hungry for another to complete it." My story needs your story, and our story needs the church's story and God's. His narrative ethics would employ cases in point. The result is a Christian morality that necessarily involves us in the story of God.[13]

Case studies can be used in preaching, according to J. Randall Nichols. They can release the energy of un-thought-about imaginery connections. They can give human form to the objective of a particular sermon. And they can heighten the immediacy of the communication of a sermon. Preachers should build concrete case histories of imaginary listeners, and then permit the listener's way of hearing and responding to be a guide to the sermon construction process.

> The case study approach is rooted in some good basic theory, which says essentially when the paths of the 'sacred story' of what we hold ultimate in existence, and our "mundane stories' of everyday life cross, in the tense atmosphere of a looming future, then you get the potential for religious disclosure, insight, the moment of the God-person encounter.[14]

The use of short plays, or excerpts of longer ones, is another way of employing the case study, not only as a resource for a sermon story but as an actual form of telling the sermon.[15]

Culture

The resources of cultural artifacts are everywhere—architecture, sculpture, archeological findings, paintings, literature, films, and other forms of life and expression. Artists provide a special resource for sermons because of their use of the imagination; their insights, too, need to be brought into radical relation with the gospel. A people's history also can be followed—exegeted—in the cultural artifacts.

Let us look at one class of cultural artifact—film—and one film in particular: *On the Waterfront*. This film, growing out of the context of the televised Kefauver Hearings and the Malcolm Johnson's Pulitzer Prize-winning newspaper articles of the 1950s, is an excellent case study of film as storytelling; we touch upon it here to suggest the ways in which a particular culture can tell its story through one form of artifact, filmworks as a parable force.[16] *On the Waterfront* is a grim story of Terry Doyle, a tool of a longshoremen's union boss, and the union's vise-grip of corruption on the New York waterfront. The union dares anyone to "sing" to the crime commission. It contains certain prevailing verbal and visual metaphors. "Pigeon" stands for more than a literal bird. One character is called a canary who could sing but not fly; he could spill information to the crime commission but was helpless when pushed off a building. Another character asks if Terry is a singer or a pigeon. Will he talk at the hearings, or will he be deaf and dumb like a pigeon? Pigeons care for each other and need tender loving care, too. But they have enemies (hawks).

The film's meaning deepens when it considers its story against certain archetypes. A useful grid is provided by Frank McConnell, who sees in film and biblical literature a model based on the seasons:[17]

Myth	Story-Type	Law	Hero	Code-Activity
Spring	Comedy	Political	Kinght	Sacrifice, clearing of the land
Summer	Romance	Civil	Knight	Civilizing, growing a garden
Autumn	Tragedy	Criminal	Pawns	Complicity, boundaries
Winter	Satire	Self-Consciousness	Foolmate	Outrage, Refounding, Courage

On the Waterfront takes place in the autumn—the "fall". Institutions have deteriorated. Criminal laws are needed. Boundaries are required. Even the church is a pawn. Framing and positioning of shots show corrupt owners sitting in high places, above weak and innocent persons in the pit. Fall is not the last word, however. Outrage converts to courage. Recognition results in renewal. The bad dies, symbolized by the closing doors in the final scene, and we know that when it opens again spring is bursting forth. Terry Doyle's sacrificial action of "clearing the land" will bring civilized laws.

One can bring specific interpretative questions to bear on this story resource: (1) Where was there guilt occurring? (2) Was there a corresponding grace? (3) Who provided the saving truth for finding new relationships? (4) Where was there a dying of an old, unauthentic way of living and an emerging new way of life? (5) Who gave a helping hand to whom? (6) How was it given?

Commentaries

This "precious" category/resource is considered last on purpose. It *should* come last, after one has surveyed the terrain on foot—or hand and foot—in search of personal observation and ideas. Commentaries should be consulted, however, since they record what wise people have thought, often collectively, about the scripture story. They are a measure against which one can set one's own understanding. The thinking of others—Barth, Brunner, Bonhoeffer, Tillich, Teihard, Taize Community—provide valuable comment.

Application

This section, like that of the preceding chapter, will illustrate how the scriptures in the two sermons of vocational calling and of families celebrating God's grace are furthered with a dialog of some specific situation in which the same biblical motifs were "hammered out" in the history and heritage, following biblical times, and preceding contemporary times.

Sermon 1, the theme of vocational calling:

St. Francis of Assisi's calling was joyful but uncomfortable. At first, the world possessed him and he reveled in material things. Upon his conversion, he truly possessed the world by stripping himself of the tangibles in which he previously trusted. He found the fullness of joy through pain and suffering. His experience was that of "tearing down" and "building up", an entry into a new Messianic time beyond chronos time.

St. Francis was an instrument of peace. His calling was to be that "mouthpiece" of love, pardon, faith, hope, light, joy. This new calling is not so much to be consoled as to console, not so much to be loved as to love. In giving there is receiving; in pardoning there is pardon. In dying there is eternal life.

Centuries stretch from his time to ours. Yet, St. Francis shows us the meaning of the biblical scriptures of the Divine and human encounter in a "Christianized" culture that has forgotten that the Lord still loves justice, mercy, and a humble walk. The principle of being chosen and choosing, of self-discovery and self-surrender, is a constant that bridges the chasm of centuries, and connects this story to our story.

Sermon 2, the theme of Christ, the water of life:

The conference assignment for this sermon was to celebrate God's grace in the less-than-perfect family life. Our goal was not to despair, but to take heart in what God does—even when the point of rejoicing seems lost. I was encouraged to be autobiographical. I hesitated for many reasons. John 4:7ff, however, speaks even to the point of hesitancy. Jesus, the water of life, is a living fountain—not for those who are perfect, the Pharisees, nor for the pharisaism within that spirit of hesitancy to speak of one's own imperfect self. Moreover, the uniqueness within my own family life is part of the point of John 4: my worship and witness need not fit prescribed categories. Grace finally takes the initiative and catches up a 19-year-old lad and a 19-year-old lass, as well as five-year-old and three-year-old boys—namely, my grandfather, my mother, myself, and my son!

Two incidents come to mind as I search my own family "roots" (between 150 and 1950 A.D.) for the point at which grace in the ordinary did occur. One was the mystery and marvel of two people who get together, my grandfather emigrating from France by himself at nineteen, finding a young woman who grew up, amazingly just thirty miles from where the message was to be given, and a third—myself—being chosen by my father to sing with him at her deathbed. To others, this may be a conjunction of strangers, a small vignette. But small things are beautiful when they grace one's life.

The second incident was the mystery and marvel of two other people who got together, my father and my mother, my mother moving at the age of nineteen, amazingly just fives miles from where the message was to be given. This was a Mennonite Conference, a people who prize family strength and biblical disciplines, and a people who "know" each other's family names, communities, and properties. But my mother was not originally a Mennonite. She was a con-firmed Lutheran. Grace seems to be blind at such points, however, and speaks for itself and through her life and her hospitalized words.

IV. THE STORY LANDS

Thesis 4: A Sermon Is Based upon a Biblical Faith-truth Plus a Subsequent Historical Faith-truth With a Present Faith-truth from the Congregational/Community Culture

Vertical exegesis was earlier defined as putting together three meaning derived from the *then* interpretation of scripture (storybook), from the *continuing* interpretation of history and heritage (past storytellers), from the *now* interpretation (storyland). Together, these searches for meaning provide a community hermeneutic for sermon research. These discovered meanings will not always occur in this order, however. One may start with one's culture (a given film) and then go to a given scripture. One may start with a pastoral problem. A relative, for intance, comments that if her niece had enough faith, she would not have suffered a mental breakdown. Then a decision is made: a sermon is needed, and the search for scripture begins. This chapter looks at four areas where one can exegete the *now* meanings.

The Priestly Area

The priestly area refers to the biblical vocation of aiding people to have rapprochement with God. It is in the word of a song to have "Just a Closer Walk with God". Evangelistic and devotional preaching have usually had this as the aim. Billy Graham and Billy Sunday have wanted to help people become Nicodemus, the converted, the one "born again". The typical devotional meditation, even at a funeral, purposes an attitude of prayer and trust. The "catholic confessional" is designed in part to assist persons to be in right relations with God. Priests want to place the hands of people into the hand of God. A central question in the priestly area is whether this match-making, this yielding up of will to God, can be done in the abstract or needs to be done concretely? Does one need to be saved/transformed generally or specifically? Observing the evangelistic meeting which may begin with preaching on the ten commandments, and also the catholic confessional, it is clear that the specific approach to priestly rapprochement with God is valid. Priestly concerns focus needs. The feeling of emptiness, for example, represents a recognized need. Anomie, or the feeling of aloneness, is a common problem identified in recent polls, as well as one of the recurring ills discovered in a study of contemporary plays.[1] Priestly sermons, however, are likely to be at their best when they confront a pastoral or prophetic of pedagogical need. One needs to experience congruence in those concerns, also.

Newness of Life

Priestly preaching deals with concrete problems in all their fullness, but it considers them as penultimate issues. An ultimate concern is newness of life. What does that mean? How is it achieved? Does it happen all at once? Does it include new dispositions, moods, attitudes, and deeds? These questions have seeded whole sets of theological writing. Our response here is to examine three related elements of priestly preaching: sensed needs, God's response, and appreciative acceptance.

A class instance of sensed need is the recognition of sin, not limited to particular actions but as an attitude that we can live without God, that in the garden of our own lives we have "enough" knowledge. This attitude results in estrangement. We see sensed need in plays like *No Exit, The Plague, Wasteland, Long Day's Journey into Night.* We behold a disrupted 20th Century in Picasso's "Guernica", Hitler's calculatd bombing extermination in Spain. See also the morning newspaper, the evening news.

Another evidence of need is our recognition of moral bankruptcy. How might this be expressed?[2] (1) It could take the shape of seeing that one has spoiled the design of things as they were meant to be. A person proud of the ability to paint discovers a bit of canvas on a wall, and paints for personal delight and applause of friends some little picture, only to discover that he has added a nonsensical or disruptive element to a vast painting of superb quality. (2) Someone states, "I'll live my own life. I don't care about others. What I do with my life is nobody's business." Later, he visits friends and family and sees what he had done to them. (3) "What a fool I've been," says the one who believes the wrong path was walked. (4) One realizes that the order of things has been offended, the "game is up"; with Peter we cry out, "Depart from me, for I am unclean." T.S. Eliot has Miss Copplestone, in *The Cocktail Party,* express our modern denial of the reality of sin as an affront to God. As the Spirit bears witness with her spirit, she says: "It sounds ridiculous—but the only word for it that I can find is a sense of sin."

Sin is public as well as private. Chicago columnist Mike Royko asks, Who killed Martin Luther King, Jr.? His answer implicated many persons.

> FBI agents are looking for the man who pulled the trigger and surely they will find him. But it doesn't matter if they do or they don't. They can't catch everybody, and Martin Luther King was executed by a firing squad that numbered in the millions. They took part from all over the country, pouring words of hate into the ear of the assassin. The man with the gun did what he was told. . . . The bullet that hit King came from all directions. . . . We have pointed a gun at our own head, and we are squeezing the trigger.[3]

The biblical concept of corporate personality, as discussed earlier, means that Adam is everyone, and that we are all in trouble. "Depravity" does not mean that we cannot do good, but that society is affected. When there is a fire in someone's home, even dry cleaning doesn't do any good. Smoke has penetrated everything—every room, every stairwell, every closet.

A second reality in the religious experience of new life is the story of God acting on our behalf. Jesus' birth, life, death, and resurrection is the supreme illustration. One example of what God's acting can mean is told by Graham Greene in his novel, *The Heart of the Matter.* He portrays an English chief of police in an African colony whose frustrations have entangled him in a web of adultery and murder. He is about to commit suicide in despair, but as a gesture of defiance he enters a church for the last time—more to damn God than to pray. There breaks upon him the awareness of one who will not let him go. The indignity of God almost disgusts him. "How desperately God must love me," he cries out. That is birth (Christmas): God thrust into our simple situation, coming where we are, subjected to the most primitive and perilous of human conditions and acting decisively to save us from sin and cynicism, death, and despair.

The metaphor of the white-robed scientists laboring in the laboratory to find a cure for disease points to the meaning of Jesus' death. Jesus grappled with the sin disease, reminds Alan Walker, and through his suffering and deformed hands we are saved, even as Marie Curie's twisted hands (as a result of the power of radium) saves us from the power of malaria. Dag Hammarskjold wrote in Easter week of 1960, "Forgiveness breaks the chain of causality because he who forgives you out of love takes upon himself the consequences of what you have done. Forgiveness, therefore, always involves a sacrifice."[4] The cross offers forgiveness. The empty cross promises power: a plus sign is upon us. We can say "no" to what dehumanizes, as we identify ourselves "dead" with Jesus on the cross, and we can say "yes" to what enhances, as we identify ourselves "alive" with Jesus in a dynamic community of faith.

A third experiential factor in newness of life is acceptance. Priestly preaching builds this into its message. Polio vaccine did little good until it was accepted. Thus, Carl Michalson, in "Communicating the Gospel," declares that preaching is not "an assertion of facts nor a simple claim to truth, a possible response to which might be skepticism. The Christian Gospel is a mobilization of decision."[5] It is an act of the will that is born out of gratitude for God's goodness, that we really belong, that we are a people with a story to enjoy and to share.

Renewedness of Life

Newness ("all things make new") does not come all at once; it is continuous. Sunday services do well to have a "call to confession", since we do not overcome the discoloring that comes to the self and society "overnight". The sad music of the heart continues to play. Our corporate guilt remains: we continue to share in an economic and social structure based on inequity and injustice. "In God we trust" seems to read, "In bombs we trust" Even the generous heart becomes proud in its generosity. Thus, the need of the devotional life, and of devotional preaching.

The Pastoral Area

"Comfort ye, my people, saith your God, speak ye comfortably." The pastoral work of the preacher is often defined as comforting the afflicted (as opposed to afflicting the comfortable). Other useful synonyms: life-situation preaching, pastoral preaching, therapeutic preaching, the psychological approach. One set of objectives for this kind of preaching includes:

1. the interpretation of human experience in the light of biblical truth rather than the exhortation of people to the observance of certain moral precepts, as such;
2. the development of personal insight into the motives of personal group action rather than the condemnation of this or that kind of behavior;
3. the encouragment of the congregation toward faith in God, in one another, and in themselves as means of gaining control over behavior that they themselves discover to be alien to the mind of Christ;
4. the growth of a sense of comradeship with God in Christ and the changing of personality through this 'transforming friendship'.[6]

So defined, pastoral preaching is both a counseling activity and a way of achieving pastoral care. It might even be called "group therapy", since it provides an opportunity for listening to, and receiving from, a source (the preacher/pastor) who is accepted by a receiver (a congregation) as a competent guide able to articulate goals and uncover resouces for the journey to maturity. Professional counselors seem to be agreed that the preaching office and pastoral counseling are similar vocational tasks, even when they are regarded as two different roles or offices.[7]

What insights can the professional pastoral counselor provide for pastoral preaching? From the "professionals" we can learn that pastoral preaching grapples with real issues emerging from our humanity. Pastor-preachers address all aspects of our psychological situation: the "confusion of youth, the disillusionment of the middle-aged, and the perplexity of the elderly". They aim, as well, to help both victims and victors in a changing society, all levels of society whether rich or poor, retarded or brilliant, student or professor, labor or management, content or discontented. Preaching arises from the same concerns with a particular point of view; "to take the needs of the people in one hand and the truth of the Christian gospel in the other and bring the two together by means of the spoken word".[8] This "brand of preachers" recognizes that people come to church to find help, and that only if the life-needs of people are met is the preacher fulfilling the preaching mission. Jesus himself recognized and served this pastoral function.

> Much of his preaching grew directly out of a practical life situation. That certainly was true of the story of the good Samaritan and that of the prodigal son. Some of his most spiritual statements were made to meet the life problem of one man or woman, such as Nicodemus or the woman at the well.[9]

Jesus' practice supports the notion that preaching is pastoral when it becomes an extension of relationships with people.

Harry Emerson Fosdick's writings and examples help illuminate the methodology of pastoral preaching; almost any of his sermons illustrates the intertwining of pastoral care and preaching. "Handicapped Lives", for instance, focuses on people's concerns and their handicaps—physical, emotional, and spiritual. Fosdick's illustrations—a crippled college graduate, Helen Keller, John Milton, Christ, Emerson, Paul—provide ample opportunity for his congregation to identify with them. He states a real problem in people's lives, about which they have been puzzled. He proceeds to examine the nature of handicaps in positive ways, such as asking how limitations might be viewed as opportunities for making a contribution to the world. The biblical story is treated with great earnestness in interpreting life's stories and to giving meaning to human experience. Fosdick's observation that a sermon's only justifiable aim is the solution of a problem has become a classic.[10]

Counseling insights should not be kept in one pocket and preaching insights in another. Donald Capps, in his quest for an integrated ministry of pastoral counseling and preaching, acknowledges that both concerns can reflect common understandings of the theory and practice of ministry. Preaching is itself an act of pastoral counseling; the two have a common theological base, and insights from psychological theories and methods clarify the communication process in preaching, Capps says.

A fruitful approach to counseling and preaching, he believes, is possible if one looks at their similar patterns and diagnosis. He suggests four such elements in their patterns: (1) identification of the problem, (2) reconstruction of the problem, (3) diagnostic interpretation, and (4) pastoral intervention. Undergirding this structural similarity is a common theological concern. Capps discovered various types which are to be addressed in sermons as well as in counseling: underlying personal motivations, the range of potential causes, the inadequate formulations of the problems, the untapped personal and spiritual resources, the lack of clarity of the problem, and the unshared human experience.[11]

The Prophetic Area

Prophetic preaching fulfills what *Godspell* defined as an appropriate goal of faith. "To love more dearly" is not enough; a more appropriate goal is "to see more clearly" so that one can "follow more nearly". Prophetic storytelling concerns itself with offering new, even confrontive, perspectives on our relationship with each other and our standing with God. Contemporary conventional wisdom of one's culture can be juxtaposed to the wisdom of the gospel, resulting—hopefully—in prophetic judgments.

A pastoral hermeneutic stresses a reading of God's grace, while prophetic hermeneutics stresses a critique of our context. As was earlier suggested, prophetic preaching is the flip side of pastoral preaching; its purpose is to afflict the comfortable. Prophetic preaching challenges today's contexts with yesterday's texts. It is the same process prophets undertook and Jesus himself used (Luke 4) in his inaugural address, when he pointed out that Elijah fed a non-Israeli widow first and that Elisha healed a Syrian leper rather than the Israelites. (This, obviously, is not without risk—since Jesus was chased from the synagogue!)

Prophetic preaching is truth meeting contemporary life and people, precipitating a state of concern. Its purpose is a saving encounter. Merrill Abbey recommends that preaching challenge the axioms of culture. The prophetic message, he writes, can be an instrument of realistic encounter with the minds to be challenged—the areas of society which are at tension with the gospel. The point of contact is discovered generally at some point of conflict. The goal here is not to find common ground, but to correct and complete the axioms or attitudes of the hearers in the light that comes from Christ.

> When deeply understood, the Bible speaks in terms of life situations so like our own that the key to incisive interpretation of the text generally lies in the discovery of the point of its challenge to the men of its own time and of ours.[12]

Effectively focusing on the point of conflict between the gospel and the assumptions of contemporary society is the key to preaching power. One discipline recommended by Abbey is to narrow the subject by bringing an aspect of the gospel into contact with a need it fulfills or an idea it contradicts, so that the two speak to each other. This struggle of defining the theme, or of narrowing the subject, he observes, is one shared also by the artist—as illustrated by Michelangelo, who asked himself many questions before he set chisel to stone. Abbey also shows how Peter's preaching at Pentecost reveals the point of contact as a point of conflict requiring a subject sharply narrowed and defined. Peter, who sensed that the bystanders had leaped to a mistaken conclusion about the excited behavior of the Christian company, used this as a point of contact: "These men are not drunk as you suppose", Acts 2:15. From this, Peter challenges familar axioms of his listeners by showing them an event in which they were involved. The result was that Peter met the hearers where they were; he made contact with their minds through symbols and ideas already familiar to them. Accordingly, he created an encounter of his hearers with God by challenging them at their motivating center of thought and life, rather than confirming them in their present thought forms.

Another method of approaching points of contact is to develop a challenge to the axioms of everyday wisdom. In the World Council of Churches study, Abbey notes that our thinking is determined largely by inner convictions, not consciously thought through, and is often expressed in the form of axioms of contemporary proverbial wisdom. Moreover, axioms are frequently at odds with biblical motifs. In an effort to identify the state of mind to which the Christian message must be addressed, national delegations at the Amsterdam Assembly attempted to crystallize axioms taken for granted in their own countries. They discovered "half-truths" which question affirmations in the Christian faith. The axioms identified by United States delegates were:

1. Truth is established only by proof, and ultimate truth is unknowable.
2. Look our for yourself. If you don't, nobody else will.
3. Human nature is fundamentally sound, but needs guidance and correction to achieve its fulfillment. "Sin" is just another name for ignorance and correctible imperfection, or biological lag.
4. There is progress in history, but society may yet destroy itself if the discoveries of science are not controlled.
5. There always have been wars and there always will be. You can't change human nature.
6. God is really a projection of man's ideals.
7. A man's religion is his own business and every man has a right to his own belief.
8. Other-worldliness is dangerous because it distracts attention from the effort to gain freedom, security, and justice in this life; and anyway, we know nothing about what happens after death.
9. Jesus was a good man. What we need are a lot more people like him. Now, take Lincoln. . . .
10. Do a good turn when you can — but don't be a sucker.[13]

Powerful prophetic preaching can occur when a scripture passage is combined with a statement of contemporary hunger that needs answering or a current attitude that needs to be questioned. To develop these disciplines, Abbey recommends the keeping of a notebook in which one writes paragraphs of a scripture and an axiom in encounter. These are "sermon starters" which will engage the contemporary mind in fruitful dialog. An update of axioms is possible if one pays attention to the assumptions of the newspaper's editorial or if one listens to or reads the latest ads.

When the Kingdom of God is presented as a radical reorganization of life, preachers are exposed to the accusation that they are "meddling". Congregations accustomed to hearing that being "born again" (or the "new reformation" of positive thinking) results in enjoying the good life, and who are conditioned to the notion that America is a Christian nation, will regard messages to the contrary as unpatriotic, unbiblical, and unacceptable. They will grumble or go elsewhere, where the image of religious "success" is popular and patriotic.

Preaching based on social hermeneutics can get preachers in trouble, especially if the focus is justice. The Social Concerns section of the Academy of Homiletics observed that preaching in North American churches generally serves the interests of the "haves", those benefiting from the prevailing political, economic, and social systems.[14] Even the emphasis of "Christianity is for everyone" is apt to endorse a "consumer" view of religion which assumes that separate versions of Christianity apply to different levels of income, education, and social place. The "equality of opportunity" presupposition ignores the reality that there can be winners only with losers. "Life, liberty, and the pursuit of happiness" stresses the Western Society's understanding of individual protection of property more than the Eastern view of human rights, equal access to education, work, health care, etc. Van Seters would have us examine our message to see if it supports those who have power and privileges against those who do not possess them. He would also have us question the preaching medium to see whether the preacher is depended upon as the great river rather than the good enabler. He would have us monitor ourselves to see whether "the banking system of education" criticism applies, with the preacher as the depositor, issuing communiqués which the congregation patiently receives. In contrast, he asks if equality of community is not more visualized when the people sit in a circle and are in dialog?

An additional way to perceive prophetic preaching is to reflect on what can be called the "radical transaction". Paul Scherer regards this view of preaching going "to the roots of human existence" of God's "relentless moving in upon our lives" and affirms the preacher's responsibility of running "the risk of becoming involved with someone in the long-continuing and God-shaped ethic of life and death". Such preaching incorporates both the history and the conflict of the gospel:

> The gospel comes to us not just as history, but as conflict. . . . It comes to us not alone as succor, but as the succor which is inseparable from demand, and in such a way that in the demand itself is the succor. . . . It comes to us not primarily as solace, an invitation to patient reliance upon God—faith is more than that—but primarily as challenge, the summons to ceaseless participation in God's creative and redeeming act, as he shares with us his own dangerous life, moving day in and day out toward the accomplishment in us and through us of his eternal purpose.[15]

John H. Patton's study of "the preaching situation" judges Scherer's radical transaction as a response to immediate and ultimate exigencies and constraints.[16]

Prophetic preaching is situational, not merely generical. The generic view examines the text, determines the main theological motif(s), and fits it into some pattern of worship. These it ought to do, but not at the expense of situational factors. The situational view takes most seriously the relationship between a sermon and the major events and experiences in a given setting, the capacities actually possessed by a particular congregation for solving pressing problems and concerns, the facilitation of resolutions of actual problems and concerns confronted by a particular congregation-as-audience. The situational perspective leads the preacher to examine the existential context and "to sense the imperfections and incompletions pressing upon the lives of persons from multiple sources as they participate in worship, to trace the presence and impact of significant values, traditions, and structures". It faces both the ultimacies in secular life and proclaims the meaning of the events in human behaviors and attitudes. Such prophetic preaching is not "just a ceremonial function" but a full participation in the ongoing drama of redemption-story.

If perchance the question remains—is controversy Christian? Or even, is Christianity controversial?—it should be noted that the question was settled long ago when the prophets spoke; in their speaking, we see that all vital questions are controversial.[17] Since prevailing values tend to make cowards of us all, everyone—laity and clergy—must repledge to "free the pulpit" and "to let it meddle". Being a prophetic storyteller does not mean standing over a congregation with a scowl. Resolution of an angry disposition is achieved in part by merging pastoral and prophetic cares, appreciating that one cannot be truly prophetic unless one is pastoral, and that one cannot be truly pastoral unless one is prophetic.

Prophetic preachers will assume the role of responsibility in raising the consciousness, of pulling back "draperies" so that *Godspell's* imperative is met – "to see more clearly". They will employ a community hermeneutic: first, in responding to the axioms and the Christ of culture mentality and, second, in working out a dialog with the experts from within and without the congregation for policies for getting a freeze on nuclear bombs and for saving the forests and the airwaves.

The Pedagogical Area

Faith seeks understanding, Anselm taught. Indeed, faith and understanding need each other. Sermons which illuminate human affair but have no roots in doctrine "shrink to cozy chats on small matters."[18] Doctrinal sermons which do not newly challenge the living human scene become arid. The task, then, is to have a moving pulpit message which releases the resources of the core of the church's faith to meet the individual and social needs of a congregation.

The first essential of pedagogical preaching is to know, oneself, the foundations of Christian faith. Preaching that would recenter people to wholeness must be preaching that knows what God has done and is doing in and with creation; it requires a theological understanding of Jesus Christ. But "pure" grasping of the kerygma is not enough. The heart of the matter is to appropriate the religious experiences which great doctrines express, which is the purpose of church doctrine. Doctrines are abstractions and thus short-hand compositions of a much longer treatise of life lived. Doctrines have some similarity to the compactness of poetry; both are built upon a lot of living. To attempt clear and relevant doctrinal preaching is to attempt the providing of the vast resources which Christian faith possesses. One way to work at this kind of preaching is the technique of "overhearing". Fred Craddock has provided a continuum of the socratic method inherent in biblical preaching and present in Kierkegaard's approach.[19] Who doesn't know the power of indirect teaching/learning that comes in eavesdropping?

A second essential for maximum understanding in preaching is the intentional use of story, and of preaching as the story of our lives. Storytelling itself produces an enchantment of theology, affirms Belden C. Lane.[20] Through story, theology remains rooted in sensory experience, stirring right-brain imagination, offering integrative healing, and providing a "truth deeper than true". The stories he suggests come from the Jewish rabbinic tradition (Akiba to the Baal Sehm Tov and Elie Wiesel) and from Christian storytellers (the Desert Fathers, Kierkegaard and C. S. Lewis). Stories from life provide an alternative way of presenting theology, different from the highly objective, analytical, and "disembodied thought which lacks the enchantment" (the in-singing) of the Spirit. Stories have always been the community teacher; they provide the context for "wising up" about life and living. Intentional sharing through story can and does occur when preaching is intergenerational, open-ended, and a shared common experience.

A third tack to a faith that seeks understanding is to intentionally teach ethics with the approach of story. Ethics is an essential component of pedagogical preaching. A holistic worship–nurture-witness is one that is socially alert and that is responding in disciplined faithfulness of the people's work in the light of God's work. True liturgy is the "work of the people". Personal and political behavior are the two sides of "whole behavior within the believing community". The essential hermeneutic for homiletics is to encounter the text in terms of desired outcomes of truth in lives of the congregation and community, i.e., in terms of ethical preaching. Corporate and communal thinking and acting are central in Christian faith.

Stanley Hauerwas, in *Truthfulness and Tragedy: Further Investigations into Christian Ethics,* remarks that character as an aspect of moral experience has been short-changed by ethics since Kant. His solution to the revival of character is the story or narrative. Character is displayed by "a narrative that provides the context necessary to pose the terms of a decision, or to determine whether a decision should be made at all".[21] "Story ethics", according to Hauerwas, has three elements. First is the awareness that moral rationality is not deductively produced from categorical imperative or utilitarian principle. Second is a world-and-life view that enables us to see how "things" hang together and to sense the importance of things. This element also helps us test the reasonableness of our judgments. Third, "story ethics" specifies ways in which we relate to each other – the different roles we can adopt. Stories are embodiments of community.

A further approach to pedagogical preaching is the use of shared experience from one's culture. Theologian Paul Tillich may have surprised some people with this view that shared experince is a more winsome form of teaching than shared belief. He recommends expressing the religious ideas in the language of contemporary society because he considers the audience as alienated from the Christian message. Accordingly, he endorses the strategies of "differentiation and transcendance". This means taking religious ideas from contexts which the audience rejects, even traditional ecclesiastical contexts, and placing them in new contexts derived from current cultural activity which the audience will more likely accept. Thus, some teachers of preaching ask students to preach doctrinally with the materials of movies and plays, rather than in religious language and concepts.[22]

Not all "stories" teach equally well, however. The critical criterion is, what kind of "world-and-life view" is taught? Some stories deny existence and, in particular, tragedy. Hauerwas emphasizes that "good stories" help us live truthfully and handle the tragedies of human life. Stories which we adopt, therefore, or which we allow to adopt us, need to possess: (1) power to release us from destructive alternatives, (2) ways of seeing through current distortions, (3) room to keep us from resorting to violence, and (4) a sense for the tragic – how meaning transcends power.[23]

The unevenness of stories available for teaching is evident from a study of mass media. George Gerbner, for instance, considers watching television to be like a form of worship. It is not only a ritual in itself, it gives us rituals (we organize meals and activities around TV) and provides us with new mytholgoies. Gerbner asks whether we have discovered the new Tribal God?[24] Similarly, Donald N. Oberdorfer, in *Electronic Christianity: Myth or Ministry,* points out that mass media tend to neglect the more painful elements of life. Secular stories such as "M*A*S*H" and "Holocaust", and church-produced stories such as "Scan" and "Insight", show that mass media can be powerful teachers – a vehicle for divine encounter, confronting us with alternatives to the human situation. Oberdorfer laments that religious mass media, as we know it, does not usually provide alternatives which lead to wholeness and renewal, so that people can alter their situations and grow into newness. He offers "sound principles" applicable to all forms of teaching by preaching: (1) an openness to human existence as it is, (2) a confrontation with those demonic elements that limit spiritual growth and human potential, (3) a reconciliation with people and with God which can lead to a divine acceptance, (4) a self-awareness that constantly deepens, and (5) a total stewardship of human life illustrating what we as created beings were truly meant to be.[25]

Application

The two previous chapters showed how sermons-research involves the use of scriptures (chp. 2) and of a story resource in which the same scripture theme was lived out (chp. 3). Now we continue with the process, and examine ways in which the story grows by coalescing insights from an exegesis of the contemporary faith experience.

Sermon 1, the theme of vocational calling:

The prophetic concern of this chapter leads us to consider the continuing need of "tearing down" and "building up". St. Francis would remind that the division of humankind into halves and have-nots still exists. Particular persons and groups that come to mind include Lech Wolensa of Poland, Hassad of Syria, participants in the Nuclear Freeze movement in the West, the "Commons" women of England, those in the women's movement, minorities, and inhabitants of the Third World. Each of these has a new leadership role in the world, much in contrast to what it was just a decade ago. A "child" or small entity will lead. It is not the "superpowers" that call the shots. Symbolic world leadership, embraced by the office of the United Nations Secretary General, often goes to a person from a small country. Dag Hammarskjold came from a nation with less population than the city of Philadelphia; his speaking and writing left his mark upon the human spirit the world over.

God still gives birth in Bethlehem, not Jerusalem. God's economics is to knock on "strange doors" and to call "unreliable" personnel in the "begats". Strength still comes out of "weakness". "His calling to fulfill" is achieved in ways unaccustomed to the unredeemed. Indeed, every valey shall be exalted and the crooked made straight. Mary still rejoices in the liberation that is coming to pass. The calling of the Third World gets first place.

Is there no value, then, in being born as one of the privileged in the U.S.A.? That question had its earlier phrasing in Romans 9. Of course, "privileges" are for ministry; privileges are opportunities—gifts to be shared. We are all called.

Sermon 2, the theme of Christ, the water of life:

Several sources from contemporary "storyland" were considered and related to the John 4:7ff text and the autobiographical materials "exegeted" in the last chapter. One source was a discussion of the nature of worship in a class at Catholic Theological Union, "Sacraments: Theology and Celebration", taught by Kathleen Hughes. From that discussion, I later saw that what is true for the appropriation of grace in worship is also applicable to family life.

A second source was Lorraine Hansberry's *A Raisin in the Sun,* which I saw performed at Goodman Theater, Chicago. The explication of love to the uttermost that Mama had her son and which was beneath Beneatha, her daughter, spoke to me with the Spirit's power. That revelatory experience of grace in the family was a gift from God's literary prophets. If it is good enough for God to use, I knew that it was good enough for me to employ.

A third source was the popular *Godspell.* The parallels to the woman at the well, particularly the question of which place and which people are "eligible" for true worship, are strikingly similar. The lyric of a response that wants to see more clearly, to love more dearly, and to follow more nearly—day by day, by day, by day—is a most eloquent statement of family transfusion and transformation.

These sources were themselves like living water poured into my consciousness. They satisfied. How shall I attribute their beckoning to me? Were they the gift of the energizing life of the Holy Spirit? Did they come to me because I "lucked out" and "got in the way" of that class, of that year's Goodman's productions, of an experience of that musical? Regardless of the how or the when, the exegesis of contemporary culture and congregation is an imperative for making John 4:7ff come to a clear and relevant message for preaching of a shared story. I'm grateful and I look forward to "putting it together" in some story form.

V. THE STORY FORMS

Thesis 5: A Shared-story Sermon is Cast into a Narrative Style and Design

Story research has produced a condensed kerygmatic statement—three horizontal theses merged into one vertical statement of good news declaration. At this stage, the sermon is like a 35-millimeter slide that needs to be projected on a larger screen so that others can see what the preacher has found. It will need amplification, clarification, verification, and simplification. Its language will need to be accurate, appropriate, interesting, and experiential. The sermon's treatment will need to be logical and psychological. It will need a beginning and an end, a design as well as a format.

Story Design

The design of a sermon serves much the same purpose as a blueprint for a building. A blueprint symbolizes what the building can be. It identifies the function, it specifies the materials that will be used, it indicates the placement of various elements. Another metaphor for such a guiding structure is a "flight path". Take-off and landing positions are marked, as well as the presence of towns and other landmarks. The classic label for structures, of course, is "outline".

However, a story's design is viewed, the following "tests" can be applied to judge its appropriateness and effect:

Completeness: both a subject and a verb are present.

Declarative: statements are in the present tense, indicative mood.

Validity: each point is true to the intention of scripture and its meaning, reflecting both larger and immediate contexts.

Strength: the issues raised are of vital concern; they are worth saying.

Expressiveness: attractive and compelling language is used.

Contemporariness: the sermon speaks to modern people; and about "us" rather than Nebuchadnezzar.

Co-ordination: the sermon's points are "parallel" in thought and feeling.

Distinctiveness: each point has something unique to say.

Movement: the points march toward a destination.

Classical/Topical Design

Several story forms can be identified in homiletical literature here with the assumption that they all have value, and as such can be "called upon" for use. The standard "shoe" typically fitted on a story is a topical one with (1) a thesis (an ordinate idea), (2) subordinate points that can be tested for supporting logic by silently supplying the word "because" or "since" or "for example" following the thesis statement, (3) several subordinate points or so-called coordinate statements that can be tested for their logic by silently supplying words "and" or "also" or "but".

The following blueprint from a story about collecting rocks as a hobby illustrates a topical design:

Thesis: Collecting rocks is a good hobby. (because)
    I. It's fun (and)
   II. It's educational (and)
  III. It's inexpensive (because)
        A. You can get a kit at the dime store for $3.75 (and)
        B. You can augment your supply from your neighbor's drive.

If the "tests" of outlining are applied as specified above, the verdict is "not too bad". Evaluate the following design. What is the "grade"?

    I. All have sinned.
        A. Adam and Eve started it.
   II. God is love.
        A. The Old Testament teaches love in the creation story.
        B. The cross is the New Testament's best sign.
  III. Come to Jesus.
        A. He is willing to save you.
        B. Only trust and obey.

Here is another example of the classical/topical story design, based upon a text covering almost two chapters. Logically, it meets the "tests" quite well. But it is a bit heavy psychologically and, actually, quite light with good news.

Title: The Trouble with Good People (Romans 2–3:20)
Thesis: All of us are "standing in the need of prayer".
Introduction: Faith-righteousness is not just for the bad guys.
    I. Good people tend to misjudge their guilt (2:1–16)
        A. Not acknowledging self-judgments.
        B. Not acknowledging proper behaviors.
        C. Not acknowledging the sliding rule of responsibility.
   II. Good people tend to misplace their confidence (2:17–29)
        A. Relying upon status.
        B. Relying upon possessions.
        C. Relying upon symbols.
  III. Good people tend to misconstrue their mission (3:1–8)
        A. Regarding themselves as "God's favorites", as "teacher's pets".
        B. Regarding themselves as having special exemption.

IV. Good people tend to misread their God (3:9–20)
A. Exempted from personal, private repentance.
B. Exempted from personal, corporate repentance.

Conclusion: We can be saved from our illusions. We are all afraid of Virginia Woolf. Here "George and Martha" are an Adam and Eve, or even the First President and First Lady; they can become a new George and Martha (Adam and Eve) and live in faith-righteousness. A special prayer will save them.

Theological Design

All sermons have some theological design. Nevertheless, this designation fits a particular method of discovering and arranging materials, as well-articulated by Milton Crum.[1] His counsel is to write a synopsis: a statement that includes a situation, a complication, and a resolution. The following example illustrates:

1. Situation: Like the rich man in the Gospel lesson, we are beset with pleas from Lazaruses for help. Like the rich man, we wish they would go away, and we refuse to give, in spite of the torment we feel when we refuse;
2. Complication: And what prevents us from giving as we should is a two-pronged fear: a fear of guilt for giving wrongly and a fear that, if we give our resources, we may become Lazaruses ourselves.
3. Resolution: However, the Epistle lesson assures us of God's perfect love for us, which casts out fear: a love which forgives us and uses our gifts, even though we give wrongly, and a love that cares for us, even when we become Lazaruses, and promises us this care into eternal life; and, in the assurance of this love, we can face the Lazaruses and make decisions about giving, free from bondage to fear.

This procedure spells out the basic theological drama of the Lazarus story in a clear synopsis. It can be further refined by breaking down the synopsis into its dynamic elements: symptoms, roots, results, gospel content, and new results. Symptom describes what is wrong, much like telling the service department something about the car or telling the doctor something about our stomach. Root explores the reasons for these symptoms. Result is the name of the outcome if we continue on the path without change or help (namely, "hell"). Gospel content is a new reading of good news for this particular story. New result is the new outcome as a result of appropriating the gospel content (namely, "heaven").

Dramatistic Design

Almost all designs have some sense of drama, a sequence of successive acts and scenes leading to a definite climax. There's some conflict or tension. Nevertheless, Eugene Lowry's "homiletical bind" has a very clear dramatic plot, an organization of thought that demonstrates a procedural interaction of problem and theme in which a basic discrepancy or tension obtains resolution.[2]

Basically, this design is an adaptation of the basic problem-solution model in which one senses some "spilled ink" on the carpet that needs to be wiped up! This profile is psychologically strong: there is a rise and a fall and a rise again. It is logically strong because it brings together the problem and the solution (the pastoral or prophetic storyland *with* the story book) in an organic and integrated way. The result is a sermon story, rather than a "lesson", designed in five stages:

1. Upsetting the equilibrium = "Oops."
2. Analyzing the discrepancy = "Ugh."
3. Disclosing the clue to resolution = "Aha."
4. Experiencing the gospel = "Whee."
5. Anticipating the consequences = "Yeah."

Lowry and Crum models have much in common with their conflict and its resolution, with their delineation of causes and outcomes, and with their call for good news. Both of them work constructively at telling the sermon story in the present tense and in the indicative mood: the gospel is about us and for us in our situation. There could be a slight temptation to "get lost" and stay with the biblical story in Crum's model and a slight temptation to "be lost" in contemporary drama with a slighted biblical story in Lowry's model. These "temptations" are not problems of the models, however. It is rather easy to call attention to "sin" with these models; because of this, a criticism has been levied that they lack joy. But their routing permits joyful topics and thankful-stories, too, such as Mary Magdalene wanting to annoint Jesus' feet (her problem).

Organic Design

An alternative to "external" forms of design is proposed by H. Grady Davis, author of *Design for Preaching*. Davis is critical of all formula designs because they may press something artificially upon scripture, and in their place he champions an organic design which grows naturally from the soil of scripture. His tree poem (which is not a poem, but a sketch of the design of an idea and of its development) is both a beautiful and a powerful expression of a sermon story that has its own roots, trunk, branches, and fruit.

A sermon should be like a tree.
It should be a living organism:
    With one sturdy thought like a single stem
    With natural limbs reaching up into the light.
It should have deep roots:
    As much unseen as above the surface
    Roots spreading as widely as its branches spread
    Roots deep underground
        In the soul of life's struggle
        In the subsoil of the Eternal Word.
It should show nothing but its own unfolding parts:
    Branches that thrust out by the force of its inner life
    Sentences like leaves native to this very spray
        True to the species
        Not taken from alien growths
    Illustrations like blossoms opening from
            inside these very twigs

> Not brightly colored kites
>> pulled from the wind of somebody's else' thought
>> Entangled in these branches.
> It should bear flowers and fruit at the
>> same time like an organge:
>> Having something for food
>>> For immediate nourishment
>> Having something for delight
>>> For present beauty and fragrance
>>> For the joy of hope
>>> For the harvest of a distant day.
> To be all this it must grow in a warm climate:
>> In Loam enriched by death
>> In love like the all-seeing and all-cherishing sun
>> In trust like the sleep-sheltering night
>> In pity like the rain.[3]

This expansion of thought begins with the sharp definition of the actual subject. A sermon on faith, for example, is not apt to be moving; "The Spirit of Thanksgiving" is broad and fuzzy; "The Character of Christ" delimits. The study of an idea's power to expand is not quickly observed because it is "a life process". To give it birth and growth, Davis poses both *structural* questions on the subject and the verb ("What is being said?" and "What is being said about it?") and *functional* questions that have to do with the thought's operation, its purpose to communicate meaning, its significance, its validity, and its consequences. (What is meant? Is it true? What difference does it make?) If one asks these five questions, an organic design is likely. If it doesn't happen, Davis suggests one more try, then going to a different passage. He recommends working with the "germinating" thrust of the verb to help a sermon design take shape. The possibilities, he sees, are a thesis supported, a message illumined, a subject discussed, or a story told. His definition of a story is an idea "embodied in a structure of events and persons, rather than in a structure of verbal generalizations, whether assertions or questions".

Story Format

Each of the sermon designs considered above constitutes a story and employs stories in unfolding their structure. Story as defined in this book means that drama of salvation which has a narrative quality in which we who were not people (without identity) are overcoming our identity crises and we who were without purpose now have a mission and ministry, and thus "the story of our lives". Hearer participants can say, "Yes, that's me; that's the story of my life, too."

Indeed, what is the make-up of the sermon-story? Literary critics usually identify three components, such as: 1) story-data (the chain of events, actions and happenings), 2) story existents (the characters — good and evil — who exert influence) and 3) story-disclosures (the means by which the content and existents are encoded).[4] Applied to sermons we can use such categories as message-plots, preacher-tellers, and preaching-events/settings. Preaching as narrative-story is an embodied structure of themes, persons and events; the result, hopefully, is a clearer life-story format. There's a growing body of literature on story-format.[5] (Applications to preaching can be found elsewhere, including the following chapter on The Storytellers.)

The heart of the story format is the metaphor of participation. Richard Jensen distinguishes this form from metaphors of illustration, wherein, once the point of the latter is discovered, the metaphor itself is dispensable. A metaphor of participation, however, is indispensable and cannot be discarded. It is integral to the message. Participatory metaphors can be both extended stories or sermons. Along with Norman Perrin, Amos Wilder, John Dominic Crossan, and others who have studied the metaphor in religious communication, Jensen sees the parable of Jesus as a series of participatory metaphors rather than as allegories. An allegory shares with the parable the simple definition of "two thoughts of different things active together and supported by a single word or phrase, the meaning of which is a result of the interaction."[6] An allegory, however, seeks to find a corresponding point of reference for every detail of the parable (the car is the donkey, etc.). The parable concentrates on a single impression or point. It is an "action-image, a bearer of the reality to which it refers". Accordingly, parabolic preaching reveals the message in and through the medium of the story.

Suggestions for story format include: (1) beginning with a text so that it is clear that the story is told in service to the text; (2) employing figures with whom hearers can identify, thus invoking the incarnational principle; (3) using one's own autobiography; (4) avoiding allegory in favor of the single-conclusion parable; (5) utilizing visual aids, thus permitting people to be more involved in solving the plot (putting the pieces together themselves); and (6) relying upon the dialogue style so people can "overhear".[7]

The latter element is especially effective in giving form to both definitions of story—story defined as part of our life, and as a specific life-story or parable of participation. Dialogue can be considered in terms of attitude or as a method. As an attitude, dialogue has been helpfully expressed in the classic writings of Martin Buber, especially *Between Man and Man* and *I and Thou*.[8] For Buber, the fundamental fact of human existence is relationships between people. The twofold attitude is expressed in the combined words-phrase of "I-Thou" and "I-IT". The difference is not in the object of meeting but in the way of relating. I-It observes, analyzes, manipulates, and uses. I-Thou meets, takes a stand in relation to, as subject to subject, self to self, person to person. Buber recognizes that I-Thou cannot be held continuously since one also becomes "a sum of qualities and images". I-It is not bad *per se*. It is undesirable when it shuts out relations that can, and ought, to be present. Genuine dialogue exists

> where each of the participants has in mind the other or others in their present and particular being and turns to them with the intention of establishing a living mutual relation between himself and them.[9]

Monologue stands in contrast to dialogue. It neither imparts oneself nor receives the other. It may, in fact, employ techniques to impress or influence, to deny or dehumanize. It is speech without interpersonal meeting. Dialogue attitudes are achievable with authenticity, presentness, experiencing the other wide, becoming aware or permitting oneself to be addressed, confirmation, freedom from aribtrary self-will, and directness.[10]

As a *method*, dialogue means more than one human voice, more than a single individual (who may, with dialogue, represent more than one person or who, by the sermon's artistry, represent a voice other than the preacher's). Dialogue of two persons, short plays, and choral readings are examples of the form now considered. A life-story, such as the extended parable, can be told with more than one person by dividing up the "script/story". It can be divided by different speakers or storytellers taking respective characters or voices, but even that is not necessary. The same character can be portrayed by two different persons; the voice of one speaker carries forward the story from the words of the other. Differing voice qualities provide a special effect that draws attention to a particular phrase, thought, feeling, contrast, or comparison.[11]

Dialogue sermons by two people embody opposite or complementary ways of perceiving. Various collections of such sermons are now available, but one can also create one's own approach, such as a medical doctor and a pastor looking at the "Christian Story of Death" on Memorial Sunday.[12] Collections of plays, either written for church use or excerpts from "secular" plays, can be utilized as an effective dialogue "introducing" a theme which then is completed with the traditional monologue.

Preachers can be imprisoned by a given form, however. "There are a number of ways to recite a paradigm in our day and in our contexts," writes James A. Sanders in his *God Has A Story, Too*. One way is the traditional monologue sermon. Others are liturgy, dance, drama, and "most of all by living thoughtfully in its reflection".[13] "If our ears are the organs of salvation," Dominic Cirincione writes in *Multi-Media Worship, A Model and Nine Viewpoints*, "God has done us a great disservice in giving us other organs of sensation and perception."[14]

The need for considering more than one format for communication, for shifting from mere lecture to the creation of an environment for discovery, was dramatically illustrated by Jesus himself. When he partially failed with words, he used visual acts in the common act of breaking bread (the congregation of two walking on the Road to Emmaus) or writing/drawing in the sand (the woman about to be stoned). When he employed both eye and ear methods, people grasped his message clearly. Certain biblical stories contain ultra-dramatic experiences such as the Old Testament prophets and kings who wore a yoke, walked about naked, became married to a prostitute, danced and built visual centerpieces. In our day, a synthesis of many arts can make storytelling a vehicle for providing equally vivid insights into relationships, patterns, and evocation. Film shorts and features encourage viewers to share in the interpretation of reality. Drama "irritates" by putting movement and action on stage and holding it there until we have a good look at it. It shows rather than talks about. It sets life before us and reveals our interior nature, thus permitting us to see our will either in conflict with the yet-to-be created or the already created which is destroying us. Great story impact is possible with such visual arts as paintings, graphics, banners, sculpture, and worship centers. Psychedelics may be out of the question, but the question that must be asked is, are worshippers ready to be taken outside of themselves—to release the forces within, and to open up to themselves, others, and God? The mixing of media and the interdependence of the media is the beginning principle of contemporary celebration and of storytelling. Communicating media and arts are available on the palette. To use them in college can be pleasantly palatable—and, more import, effective storytelling.

Application

This section takes the research findings from Chapters II, III, and IV and integrates them into one vertical exegetical thesis, showing what might result in an etched (outlined) story-sermon. The "tests" cited in this chapter were run on each outline to discern if it had logical and psychological validity. The points grew out of one central kerygmatic faith statement. Together they serve as a blueprint for a "building". And yet, "building" is not quite the precise metaphor:

it is more of a flight plan, and thus a narrative journey—hopefully, a faith story, one that you and I share, along with God the co-pilot.

A written manuscript, an approximated "oral manuscript", a message for the ear rather than for the eye, appears in the next chapter.

Sermon 1, the theme of vocational calling;
> Title: "Who's Calling?"
> I. Calls interrupt.
>> A. We're ambivalent about phone disruptions.
>> B. We've reasons for our ambivalences.
>>> 1. There are fearful calls.
>>> 2. There are annoying calls.
> II. Calls name/claim us.
>> A. A name identifies us.
>> B. A name intimates us.
> III. Calls summon/invite us.
>> A. They appoint us.
>> B. They move us out.
>> C. They give us vocation.
> IV. Calls lay expectation on us.
>> A. They are purposive.
>> B. They ask a response.
> V. Calls offer opportunity for a tentative closure.

Sermon 2, the theme of Christ, the water of life:

Whoever said that sermons must have three points probably based it upon empirical observation. What one must say is that sermons must have *one* point, and that sometimes that point needs some additional amplification or verification with some "becauses" or "for examples". How many of those subordinate points are necessary depends on the subject, its complexity, and the audience's knowledge of that subject. Nevertheless, there is a limit to what people can remember without taking notes, let alone the storyteller's remembering power and prowess. The previous sermon, a more typical "Sunday morning one", has five points but the first one is like a "take-off" for a plane and the final one is a landing strip for some "flight".

Because the following sermon is designed for a conference sermon and because it was assigned, it lends itself more to a "topic to be discussed". At least, that's my justification of six points.

> Title: "Grace, Where Are You?" (or "God's Grace and Our Families")
> Introduction: "Do gold faucets and 42 phones a happy home make?" Are graced homes the result of lucking out?
> I. Family grace comes as a gift.
>> A. Marriage and family are gifts.
>> B. The magnetic power of love is a gift.
> II. Family grace comes in the orindary.
>> A. It comes while one is about one's chores.
>> B. It comes in the here and the there of family histories.
> III. Family grace comes as a process.
>> A. It comes in progressive increments.

B. It comes in biting tongues and biding time.
C. It comes in extended families.
D. It comes in staying on.
IV. Family grace comes in recognition of being a loved sinner.
    A. It comes in a radical consciousness of a unique adoption.
    B. It comes in not-so-precious memories.
 V. Family grace comes in being loving servants.
    A. Graced nuclear families explode into sharing with extended families.
    B. Graced families discover the servanting of communication.
VI. Family grace comes most and best when one is in a Godspell.
    A. It is a heterogeneous group.
    B. It occurs not in *a* place or by special initiations and rituals, but in a special sanctuary called family.

VI. THE STORYTELLERS

Thesis 6: A Sermon Is Prepared and Presented by Convinced Preacher and Congregational Storytellers

In order to clarify the roles of participants in worship, Soren Kirkegaard drew a direct analogy with dramatic constructs. We act as if the preacher and the choir are the actors and the congregation the audience. God's bit is to serve as a prompter for the actors. However, the way it really is, God is the audience. The congregation serves as actors. The preacher and the choir prompt the congregation to do its rightful thing. Kirkegaard's points are valid, even though his categories are not as discrete as they could be. It is more accurate to realize that all three groups (God, congregation, and pastor and choir) serve interchangeably; each, at times, is actor, prompter, or audience. In this chapter, we will explore the role-taking of two of the three participants—preacher and congregation—in the task of preaching as shared storytelling.

The Preacher As Storyteller

> I never see my rector's eyes,
> He hides their light divine;
> For when he prays he closes his,
> And when he preaches, mine!
> Anonymous

"The eyes have it" in storytelling, but they don't have it all. The total psychic life of the preacher is involved in effective preaching, according to a pastoral psychotherapist.[1] The content of the pastoral message is qualified by the preacher's dreams and fears, loves and struggles. Emotional life, fantasies, and relationships with family, parish, and God are all part of the preaching "act". The communication process always involves the question of whether the preacher believes the story. It raises other questions as well. In what ways is the message shaped by the preacher's own intrapersonal and interpersonal conflicts? What connection exists between the message and the preacher's skills, charisma, and caring? How convinced is the preacher of preaching as shared story?

Psychologically, the preacher has to be in tune with the message-story. The preacher says about this creation, "It is good." It may not have fully arrived but it is in process. "It points in the direction that I, too, want to go and grow. I can emphathize with the sermon motif: this is the way it is sometimes—and with me. It is, in fact, bone of my bone, and gut of my gut."

Intellectually, the preacher has to have confidence in the message-story. It is based upon a sound, solid kerygmatic statement. It isn't "musty" (you must do this, you must do that), but it is "gutsy"—a declarative slice of goods news. It reflects a biblical passage that has been re-searched, that has been lived out in history and heritage, and that is now being tested in the lives of people today. The sermon is a coherent whole, with a progression that follows a route that can be committed to memory. It is an oral manuscript—it can be talked through as a dialog.

Devotionally, the sermon story is a prayer, a living offering presented with eyes wide open to the mercies of God. It is the first and most recent fruits "of my labors" and therefore an obla-tion. It is delivered with the prayer that it serve as a vehicle that can prompt others to ponder anew what the almighty can do, that the sermon will be a channel for people to tune into and re-late their own experience and add their own perceptions. The prayer is that God will transcend the limitations of this art-piece and create a new thing(s). With this sermon goes a prayer: "I believe in synergy, that $1 + 1$ equals more than 2, help my unbelief."

Confessionally, the sermon has a living center and, therefore, is a story.[2] It isn't about the whole Bible, but about one aspect that involves God, the church, society, the congregation, and the preacher. As a literary form, the sermon-story is respectable. It isn't just re-telling some-thing about the Corinthians; it is also an imaginative recasting for our time. It involves active lis-teners who are not only participants in the act of storytelling but in the process of their own be-coming, in light of the good news. They will listen and, like King David listening to Preacher Nathan, ask, "Who is that guy?" only to find out that they have met him. If the message at times seems indirect, if the congregation has a sense of eavesdropping, no harm is done; what the lis-tener needs most is not "more information" but "more commitment". Christ, who often walks incognito among people, can be a surprise-guest this way. It isn't necessary for the preacher to give the "only" definitive moral of the story.

Rhetorically, however, the preacher as a participant uses the discipline of storytelling. It is the responsibility of the preacher to acquire skills that make the story effective:

- The sermon should be blocked out in acts like a drama, or in outline form, or in some sequence of action phases.
- The beginning, or at least one "start" of the story, should be memorized.
- The sermon story should be visualized; think in terms of vivid picture words to enhance the process of communication.
- Delivery of the story should be practiced, with special attention to:
  (a) looking at the entire audience/congregation, rather than at one person or one area;
  (b) speaking in a natural but an adequately projected voice;
  (c) using a variety of inflections and a varied rate, particularly on key words and feel-ings;
  (d) employing direct disclosure, putting a number of things in quotation marks;
  (e) monitoring meaningless movements, such as handling beads, bracelets, collars, pockets, watches, rings, money, ears, noses, hair;
  (f) tape recording the final delivery and playing it back to identify things that worked well and things that need work for next time.

Charisma

Pentecostals remind us that charisma is fun, and politicians that it is true. But at times it is neither: Hitler and Mussolini, who governed by the force of emotion and charisma, prove that special ability to stir blood is, necessarily, neither health nor grace. They remind us that there is a darker side to the power to rule by strength of personality or persuasion. Social analysts point out that leadership is dependent upon those who would be led. Before there is a crusade, there must be crusaders; before there can be a Moses, there must be a people of Israel who want freedom from the bondage of Egypt. Charisma waits not just for the person but for the purpose.[3]

What, then, do we do with charisma? We all have charisma, a deep and powerful influence on other human beings. We have a personality, a flame of selfhood by which we respond to life. We cannot hide from it just because we do not wish to stir up people's passion, attract followers, have extraordinary experiences or attention. The Pentecostals are correct in asserting that God's spirit dwells in us and speaks through our charisma, that the Holy Spirit acts on us and that we react with our charisma. The courage to preach comes as God's spirit speaks to and through us.

Charisma is a particularly useful word when defined biblically, not as charm, magnetism, mystique, persuasiveness, capacity to excite and inspire, but as a gift owned and possessed by all of the people for all of the people. Like *agape,* charisma is a Christian word; it means grace, God's presence, help when weak, forgiveness when sinning, hope when in despair, joy when sad. Charisma flows from God's grace. It is an endowment of the Spirit which can take many forms. In the light of biblical principles, charisma is given to all who believe and is not the possession merely of a small elite — which apparently means the most dynamic preacher has no more charisma than the one who sews for the hospital or sings in the choir. Charisma is exercised for the service of others rather than for self-glorification, personal vanity, or out of rivalry. And charisma is a gift to be sought, found, and exercised, rather than that which happens or is ignored. Since some are given the gift of preaching, the preacher's concern is to exercise charisma as an instrument of the sermon.

Commitment

Commitment is another factor enabling the preacher to get the message to the congregation. Effective preaching requires a person who is committed to Christ and the church, and who is led by the Holy Spirit. Jesus came preaching in the power of the Spirit giving evidence of an awareness of being rooted and grounded in God's power, which was at work in him and in the contexts where he preached. Commitment ignites passion for forthtelling truth. James A. Forbes, Jr., in asking why preachers are Holy Spirit shy, answers that our secular and scientific technological times apparently make one feel that it is inappropriate, and that preachers do not want to be viewed as those having spiritual exhibitionism. But soft-pedaling the place of the Holy Spirit, he argues, works against our diligence in seeking the empowerment and guidance fo the Spirit.[4] Commitment, insists Kyle Haselden, comes in part through confidence in the urgency of the message, in recapturing the vision of peril and promise biblical motifs in human experience.[5] In the rediscovery of the call to be totally involved in the will of Christ and under the authority of Christ in preaching, Haselden says, the Word regains confidence in the preacher her/himself. Commitment to other facets of the preaching task is also integral, including empathy with the people and a grasp of their problems, crafts in composition, and training in the power of the spoken word.

Communication

Developing communication skills is the fourth consideration for storytelling. The ability of the preacher to tell a story, and not the content of his message, is the critical question in the people's inquiry of every minister, according to James Cone.[6] In his discussion of "The Story Context of Black Theology", Cone illustrates how the theme of liberation is expressed in story form. He notes that blacks have appropriated biblical stories to meet this historical need, stressing some themes and stories while overlooking others. Black theology, Cone writes, embodies the story of a people's struggle for liberation in an extreme situation of oppression. The force-power of the story in that struggle, he maintains, is "embodied in the *act* of telling itself". Ultimately, form and content are in dialectical relation, the story serving both as the medium through which the message is told and as a constituent of the truth. The greatest emphasis on storyteller, however, affirms the reality of liberation to which the story points as also being itself revealed in the actual telling of the story. "Through the medium of stories, black slaves created concrete and vivid pictures of their past and present existence, using the historical images of God's dealings with his people and thus breaking open a future for the oppressed not known to ordinary historical observers," he writes.

Cone's concerns concur with Henry Mitchell's, who reminds us that one of the characteristics of an effective preacher who "gets through" to the congregation is the ability to tell stories.[7] As earlier noted, the preacher as communicator is one who "tells" well. Specific skills in storytelling include the ability to visualize the story in the mind, blocking the story in acts like a drama, in sequence of action phrases. Vocal skills include variety of pitch, rate, and volume, natural pauses, and a voice quality that is natural and resonant (see Appendix 4 for additional disciplines). Visual skills reinforce words: sights and sounds are teammates.

Preachers can accommodate themselves to the relativity of words, not as things in themselves but as symbols of experience, valid when they are mutually accepted and understood.[8] This requires that one knows the idiomatic language of the moment in the culture in which one is preaching so that the symbols can be mutually accepted and understood. F. Thomas Trotter regards preaching discipline in a similar light to that in which Paul Valery viewed poetry: as "willed inquiry, subtleness of thought, the soul's assent to exquisite constraints, and the perpetual triumph of sacrifice".[9] Preachers should emulate the poet, whose language is that of the vernacular in its most economical shape through striving for the most precise and accurate statement, phrase, or word.

The poet's gift of imagining also assists the preacher, since poetry is the translation of the perceived image into words of experience. Imagination, according to Trotter, is "the ability to perceive connections, to see profounder relationships that lie in the common events of our lives. To listen and look before speaking, to frame our words so carefully that they themselves have a sacramental character, so that there's a translation between God and the worshipper." Effective preaching requires language that is accurate, appropriate, interesting, and experiential, in addition to requiring skillful use of vocal and visual communication skills.

Caring

The ability to care also is a distinguishing characteristic of the preacher as storyteller. Caring for another person is to help the other grow, to aid the other in finding wholeness without imposing one's own direction. It is to invite the other to care for something or for someone apart from him or herself, or to help find or create areas of one's own life in which one is able to participate in caring relationships for oneself.[10]

This "helping relationship" has three central ingredients: (1) accurate empathy or sensitivity to what the other person is experiencing and communication, (2) nonpossessive warmth or acceptance of the other as a person apart from any evaluation of his/her behavior or thoughts, (3) genuineness or meeting on' a person-to-person basis, without defensiveness or retreat into a facade or roles.[11]

Caring is not acquiescence. As both pastor and prophet, the preacher must seek a creative tension between the art of caring and the act of prophetic confrontation.

Credibility

Credibility is a characteristic of communication that cuts across other attributes. According to Aristotle, good communicating results from being a good source. More contemporary research into this subject suggests that no single factor controls the "goodness" of a source, but that credibility is a set of perceptions held by the receivers. Among these perceptions are the notions of safety, qualification, and dynamism. A speaker is "safe" if he/she is congenial, forgiving, fair, hospitable, cheerful, patient, and gentle. Training, experience, and intelligence enhance the perception of qualification. A dynamic source is aggressive, emphatic, and direct.

There are a number of ways to achieve credibility and to maintain it once it is established. Credibility can be improved, for instance, by the way a speaker is introduced. First impressions are important, even those before one begins preaching. Organizational status becomes an element of credibility, once it is known. Openness to different kinds of information, and passing those experiences along, helps create a bond of credibility between preacher and congregation. "Revealing" one's voluntary membership can indicate the set of attitudes a communicator has. Identifying the beliefs and attitudes of the audience and building them into the message, using authorities respected by the audience, and adapting one's message to the largest number present, are other avenues to increased credibility.[12]

The People as Storyteller

It's obvious that preaching cannot be performed in isolation and that a shared story calls for more than a speaker. Preaching requires the context of a community of faith. This community provides a seedbed in which the partnership of Spirit, preacher, message, and congregation—each according to its talents and role—results in the flowering of a new community and a deepened faith.

Regrettably, religious communication theorists and practitioners generally ignore the role of the congregation in this partnership of storytelling. If a congregation had the opportunities to speak, what would a preacher hear? According to Edgar Jackson, a preacher who emphasized the pastoral, he would hear the murmurings of hope, the cries of illness, the overwhelming silence of guilt and doubt.

Jackson suggests that one visualize the congregation's needs in sermon preparation. In a congregation of five hundred people, he writes, a preacher would assume the following needs:

one-half would be feeling of acute sense of loss from bereavement; a third of those married would face personality adjustment; another 50 per cent of the whole would have problems of emotional adjustment to either school, work, home, or community. Others would likely have neuroses due to alcohol addiciton or other obsessions. An approximate 15 would likely be homosexually inclined and 25 would be depressed. About 100 would likely suffer from deep guilt feelings. The congregation's actual stories, if heard, would come from persons "burdended with sin, fearful of life and death, injuring themselves by pride and jealousy, or making life miserable for others through resentments and masked hatred".[13] These stories need converting so that these same people have a sense of forgiveness, a living faith, a self-understanding, and good will. Although the sermon story that the preacher shares can be soul-healing, it will be soul-injuring if it sets false goals, stimulates unhealthy resentment, promises an unreal security, or encourages submissiveness or aggressiveness.

Preaching need not be a banking system of communiqués patiently received by the audience.[14] George Buttrick argues against the preacher telling "his" story oblivious of the story in the minds of the congregation (in his Yale Lectures on Preaching, Auburn Lectures, Rall Lectures, and Belden Noble Lectures).[15] Focusing on the congregation's stories, his classes on preaching covered how to preach to the present age—the humanist, the existentialist, the agnostic, the Marxist, the doubter, the anxious, and even the biblical person. Buttrick, who took seriously his audiences, wanted them to know that they were heard. He desired that the congregation itself would confront the devil (insisting that "we" are both Dr. Jekyll and Mr. Hyde). He let them come to the conclusion that they could not save themselves ("We can't send the Hiroshima bomb back into the sky . . . there is no return ticket."). He let them sense that only God can heal ("God doesn't make bargins with the devil . . . Calvary is not a patch on a blunder, but a light flung back on all creation."). He was eager for the people to be receptive to God and to neighbor ("If we fail to forgive we end up freezing out God's love."). When compared with the pastoral-prophetic preaching of Edgar Jackson, George Buttrick's was more prophetic-pastoral. But both wanted the people heard; both enabled the congregation to be active participants in the drama-story of salvation.

The People Speak

Can congregations speak? Do they know what they themselves need or want? Do they recognize a good storyteller if they hear one? One study of "Lay Expectation Factors in Religion to the Preaching of Helmut Thielicke" responds in the affirmative.[16] It shows the laity in substantial agreement on the importance of eight factors in the sharing of a sermon, ranked in this order: credibility, practical help for living, use of the Bible, theological content, comprehensibility, relevancy, confrontation with decision, and thought provoking. In addition, the listeners "knew" they were being given help to meet their needs. They were aware of "dialog" between pulpit and pew. (Those who were aware of a high degree of dialog in Thielicke's preaching were also more aware of having their needs met.) The listeners were positively affected by the preacher's credibility. Where credibility was high, and where the laity was consciously concerned with content, then style and format were of less concern.

The study identified elements in the success of Thielicke as a preacher, which related specifically to his ability to fulfill his audience's expectations. These elements and expectations were: his boundless energy, thoroughness in sermon preparation, use of the textual-thematic method of organizing and developing a sermon, his broad background in theology and ethics, his ability to give the biblical message contemporary significance, his way of confronting people with the necessity for making decisions, his ability to preach from a manuscript without giving the impression that he was reading, his practice of including the congregation in his thoughts by his use of the pronouns "we" and "you", his practice of not separating diagnosis and analysis from the remedies and solutions, his ability to analyze problem situations, and his constant and continual effort in writing.

The People Respond

The congregation can also participate in storytelling in a direct way: it can be involved in the planning, presenting, and practicing of preaching. A recent wave of literature has addressed this how-to-listen need.[17] Talk-back sessions have been added to the list of options available for lay participation. The Pastoral Institute for Advanced Studies in Michigan, under the direction of Reuel Howe, developed a series of questions that a small group could process as they discussed the sermon and made available their comments to the preacher.

Howe's talk-back sessions have been replicated many places. Following attendance at the Institute, a "Yes, but . . . " discussion hour was established. Three questions were considered:

1. What did we hear, experience, understand (Clarification)?
2. What do we believe as a result of this sermon/service (Consensus)?
3. What do we propose to do about it, how follow up (Commitment)?

Many of the sessions required the entire time to walk through the first question, especially on such sermons as "Selma, Saigon, and Salvation". Each step is invaluable to both preacher and congregation. They are integral for functioning as storyteller.

Corporate storytelling requires finding appropriate methods for preparing, presenting, and practicing the sermon-stories. One effective way of doing this is through *ad hoc,* special task force, or regular worship committee. Such a group works a four-fold process of preparing the storytelling.[18]

1. Pressure Points and Preoccupations: It is important to ask specific questions, such as, what are the most important areas of one's life, where one comes most fully alive, most wholly oneself? What does one really want and where is one pressed most to live most? Pressure points and preoccupations guide one's private prayer life, so why not also the public? To take these "points" seriously in worship is to affirm that a congregation's history is meaningful, the struggles are worthwhile, and to attest that the Spirit of God leads now in the "way of truth and life". This is a phenomenological step which exegetes the lived-moments of human existence and experience. Step one is to ask in a supportive small group such leading questions as, "Why did we wake up last night (other than because of the alarm clock)?" "What bothers us in today's news?"

2. Etiological Explications: After we have named the symptoms, we need to identify the causes. That is the approach we use when going to the medical doctor, the garage, the gripe session concerning our favorite team's losses. Accordingly, the small group seeks to understand causes for their preoccupations and pressure points. *Why* does this or that bother us? *Why* do we wake up with these concerns? When a patient says, "If I only knew why . . . ", she/he is saying that part of the answer is to know the reason why the problem exists. Although easy compliance and peace-of-mind heresies may find this step too sandpaperish, honesty demands the

radical processes of going to the roots. Loving the Lord God with wholeness of heart presupposes hating the false gods. Such loving necessitates knowledge.

3. Good News: The group approach methodology asks next, what new ways are there for looking at the things which bother us? Is there some way to break the old patterns? Small groups can engage in the gift-giving of insight. The group facilitates pilgrimage as "one beggar tells where there is food" and then another joins. Such food may be some recently appropriated scriptural meanings—by one of the members or by the small group itself. The resourcefulness of a resident theologian (the local preacher/pastor) should be helpful. But good news is not restricted to the Bible. A challenging book, appreciated nature, a story family experience and break-through, a movie, may provide a new insight that will break the "hold". Out of the repertoire of a small group, some sturdy shoot (like a small trunk of a tree) will emerge. It should be prized: it is a facet of the Word of God, something that proclaims the way the group can go in its corporate life-story.

4. Available Signs: The fouth step of small-group storytelling is ascertaining the modes of lifting up the good news for the causes of the symptoms. Now it is timely to inquire whether the story form be that of a sermon, a song, a banner, a litany, slides, sculpture, drama, etc. These "arts" become the people's way of responding and of telling their story. They embody elements of human existence, experience, and expectation. This kind of small-group storytelling can provide dramatic insights into the needs and concerns of the congregation at large.

In one instance, as volunteers in a joint parish in a Chicago suburb proceeded through these four steps, they saw that their remarks were remarkably diverse; they lacked oneness as a congregation. They were "so different". As they mused over this, it seemed natural to identify some of the causal factor: differences in color, culture, community background, expectations, roles, wealth, age, and education. They then groped for an organizing principle for the church—for *their* church—and came to consider the concept of "the body" (all for each, each for all, as in I Corinthians). The next step was to consider which story forms could be used to lift up their life for confession, correction, and consecration in worship. One person volunteered her junior-high class for making a banner. Although meant for a throw-away after a week or two, the banner lasted several months in active use. No wonder: on one side, its seven faces illustrated the types within their congregation and the words, "The Church Divided Falls"; on the other side were the same faces with the caption, "Together in Christ, the Church Understands". One member wrote a litany, "Unity in Diversity". The morning service had a short sermon followed by a layperson's critical response.

Another small group came to the conclusion that they were not clear as to the mission of the church. Many families had moved out of the neighborhood because of integration. The sermon they developed, as they worked through the four steps of group storytelling, was a role-play dialog between two members who "were shopping in the local grocery store" with one a "remaining" member and one who had "moved". The sermon's introduction was, "Well, how are things going over at the church now?"

Another group began their "conflict" over the breakdowns of communication with children, parents, spouses, employees, employers, neighbors.

Still another group realized that they did not have time to come out to this small group's meeting, even though they had signed the clipboard as volunteers to meet. Their theme, understandably, was time. One member's litany ended with the question, whether we worship and kneel at the clock or the cross?

A similar procedure was tried by a church in Ohio, using a confessional liturgy in which pastor and people shared openly in their faith struggles and faith experiences.[19] "Celebration Planning Groups" selected themes for the sermon and the worship service by sharing recent experiences, questions, or concerns. One experience would trigger a similar experience or question from another. As the group shared, a trend or direction developed and a theme was selected. Subsequent meetings discussed what might be said about the theme and how the message would be presented. The group took responsibility for planning the order of worship, determining the progression of the service, and the worship within each section. Participants often assumed actual leadership in conducting the worship service. The primary value of the Celebration Group was that of worship growing out of the life-experiences of the members, and the "built-in guarantee that this worship will directly relate to their lives". The hymns were ones which had meaning to them, the thoughts which called the people together in worship, and the statements of confession were their expressions, the theme the result of their questions and concerns.

The congregation also had "Worship/Preaching Groups" consisting of invited members meeting on Tuesday evening, for four weeks, in groups of six to ten. Each meeting began by reviewing the last Sunday's worship. Questions asked were: What did you find helpful and what served as a hindrance in your worship? What were both the most and the least meaningful parts? The second function of the group was to look at the next Sunday's worship by a study of the scripture text. Discussion questions included: What questions do you have regarding this passage? What problems does it raise in your mind? What do you undertand to be its meaning? How has this biblical truth found expression in your life? In what ways can you witness to its reality?

The entire process gave church members an opportunity to evaluate the worship and give their critical and supportive feedback; it gave them a sense of greater "ownership" of the worship service, and resulted in a greater eagerness for the worship on the part of the participants, as they anticipated the ways in which their ideas and input would be used. The discussions also kept the preacher in touch with the questions and experiences of the members.

What can be learned from the way the people responded in these several "experiments" near Chicago and in Ohio? What do they say as a congregation uses small groups as storytellers on behalf of and for the entire congregation?

1. Liturgy's meaning, the work of the people, affirms the congregation as storyteller.
2. A group's stories involve the total person, mind, emotions, myths, will.
3. Stories celebrate human experience, joys, and concerns, in light of the faith.
4. Worshippers have the right to focus on the events and feelings that they have been experiencing as well as to corporately and interactionally anticipate what can follow in subsequent worship experiences.
5. Story building can use a series of steps, such as phenomenological sequence of identification, understanding, new perspectives, and symbolization.
6. A small group is a natural storyteller.
7. Storytelling utilizes the arts and media as means of "connecting".
8. Laity need guidance in the experience of the priesthood of all worshippers.
9. Corporate stories work for integenerational worship.
10. Congregational storytellers need to "tell" in some such fashion as shown here, at least occasionally, perhaps once a month. The preacher as storyteller has some great assistants to help tell the stories.

Applications

The two sermon scripts that follow are the result of the homiletical steps of previous chapters and the insights of this one. The first sermon was given to a congregation, a pastor's conference, and a curriculum committee on education and worship. The second was presented to the Illinois Mennonite Conference.

Sermon One

Who's Calling?

Jeremiah 1:4–19; Romans 9:20–26; Luke 4:16–20
by LeRoy E. Kennel

"Can you take a phone call?" Pauline yelled, as I struggled with the just-started, difficult-to-run lawn mower.

"Well, maybe, who is it?"

The phone's disruption, its ringing annoyance, is offset by the recognition that someone wants to talk to us. That calls bother us is understandable. We are disrupted. Recently in a strange town I put nonleaded gas into my car instead of diesel; I called what appeared to be the only garage open that evening and was told, "I really can't talk now since I'm the only one here and I'm painting a car."

We know that sometimes we get bad news. Nevertheless, when we go away from home, do we "hide" our phone number? Do we not tell people where we can be reached, and do we not check the bulletin boards where such calls are listed?

Bad news was a reality one February afternoon. The operator said, "Go ahead, there's your party." And then, "LeRoy, this is Lester. (pause) How's the weather?" I waited, knowing that the weather was not the call's purpose. Another pause, and then, "Mom passed away after lunch — in her own chair."

Sometimes the phone call is just annoying. "This is an advertising program and you have been selected. . . . We would like to stop by and explain. Would 8:00 P.M. be all right?"

Sometimes, it's sinister, like the program following the 10:30 evening news. The phone rings and the voice on the other end says, "You are visiting your mother, right? You should be home; something is going on there that is not very nice. This is a friend who wants you to know that your spouse is cheating on you."

And then sometimes there's that recorded message: "I'm sorry but no one is in the office at this time, but when you year the sound on this 'monster,' you may begin your message."

But regardless of our responses, our ears are alert to the phone's ringing. We hasten with the unlocking of the door if we hear it ringing. We ponder and wonder, "Who's calling anyway?"

Indeed, who *is* calling? The telephone is a metaphor of the calling experiences in the Bible? Do we really need to ask who was calling Jeremiah to the ministry? Who was calling Israel to become a people of God? Who was calling Jesus to fulfill the messianic promise? Who was calling Paul to be minister to the Gentiles? Or who is calling each of us?

There is but one answer. "I am who I am: I am the Lord your God who brings you out of your own Egypts, who leads you to the land of fulfillment, who delivers you from your various enemies, who prepares a table before you, and who leads you into righteousness. And I am the one who makes you a mouthpiece, too."

"I, God, call you, person-to-person. Are you there? Can you take a call?"

Well, just what is the call about? The biblical word for call, *kaleo,* is used both as noun and verb. These two literal uses have their correponding nonliteral uses. Both sets of meanings become opportunities for deeper meanings in biblical faith. The noun use answers the question of what the call concerns. The noun use is to give a name. God called the light *day* and the darkness *night.* (Gen. 1:5) "You shall call his name Jesus, for he will save . . . people" (Mt. 1:21). At the local animal clinic, they asked me, "And what is your dog's name?" I proudly answered, "Peaches." This naming dimension is one of identification, of relationship.

The second noun meaning, the faith thrust dimension, is that of claiming by naming. Abram becomes Abraham. Jacob becomes Israel. Simon becomes Peter. The Lord addresses Israel, "I have called you by name, you are mine" (Is. 43:1). The zenith of claiming by naming is, "Behold, what manner of love [God] hath bestowed upon us, that we should be called the [children] of God" (1 Jn. 3:1).

The caller God, as evident from Romans 9, purposes our election, coming not as a result of our good deeds but because of God's good calling, even as understood by Hosea, those who were without identity, who were "no-people," are now "my-people," and she who was not beloved is called "my beloved."

Can I take a call? Are you kidding, when the call is about a Good Shepherd who knows the sheep by name, who gives an identity, who salutes by title, who takes the initiative in identifying me and inviting me to the party of all times?

Another quite natural question is, "What's wanted?" This answer is a matter of hearing the verb use, that of summoning. We are invited to step out from behind so that we can see more. The prophets, it seems, were always inviting others to "see more clearly." The call can mean for us something similar to Abraham moving out of his favorite niche—Ur of Chaldees—to another locale where one is less sure of oneself. It can mean going with Moses to some burning bush where God's presence is unmistakable, or to the very top of Sinai where one knows a covenant or where a new commandment will be given. We are invited with Hosea to be wooed and won by God into a wholeness program, of both mind and emotions.

Another dimension of the verb meaning is that of commissioning. We are invited with Isaiah to see and seek God in the history of the nations and not just our people. It is going with Jesus and the early church to bring release to captives, to give sight to blind, and to enable the lame to walk, and to give liberty to the oppressed. The commissioning is not to be silent but to say, "Here I am, send me." It is not to die but to lay down a life. This commissioning is nothing less than adopting a new vocation (even though it may occur within the old job).

With Jeremiah we will need to translate and transmit into our own international forebodings just what it means "to tear down" and "to build up." For some that may well mean scrutinizing the nation's patterns of solving security with nuclear bombs. Some will hear the call to tear down false security blankets of MXs and Pershing missiles. Some will hear the call to build up universities of peace studies instead of colleges of war. Some congregations will create a peace center which will be available for the church and the community, possibly a booth at the county fair. All of us ought to hear a discrepancy between "American with strength" (via military weapons) and "inherit the earth" (via gentleness).

With Jesus we will need to reinterpret and reapply Isaiah 61 in our own synagogue readings. In the mid-1960s, for example, we saw, with Paul, that the channels (the ceramic pots) which were reserved for special people (such as seating for whites in buses) and for special occasions are now for everyone and for everyday tasks. We came to see that those who were "no-people" have become "first-class, first-place" citizens. What are we called to see 20 years later? Are we not called to witness against a new "me" generation? Are we not called to work for evangelism and church planting?

In every age the Eternal Voice will be heard to say, "Justice, mercy, and humble walk are still in vogue." With St. Francis we will question the expensiveness of clothes that result in depriving the have-nots. "Haves" and "have-nots" is a particular problem for "Christian America." Apparently, the Catholic bishop's statement on economics is a call to us—real and personal like a telephone call from God. When Pope John Paul II in his pre-Christmas sermon called the Soviet prison camps a form of slavery, and then went on to call Western consumerism "also slavery," is this not something to be pondered?

It is appropriate that we hear the Helsinki Watch report, "Tears, Blood, and Cries—Human Rights in Afghanistan Since the Invasion 1979–1984," which condenms the actions of Soviet troops. It is also proper for us to evaluate Pope Paul II's words that "in the civilization of the rich countries, where there is not only a practice but also a mentality of consumerism, each person can become a slave of this system of life."

Christmas is now past, but what of the joy that came to the church? How are we called to embody joy energy? Do not Helen Keller's words still suggest, "The best way to be grateful for one's sight is to help someone in the dark"?

Jesus' inaugural address (Luke 4 in whic he aligned himself with Isaiah 61) is a call to embody mercy and incarnate joy. Those who follow Christ, who would be nicknamed "Christians," will study how the Christian mission works itself out in this new year.

Two familiar statements are particularly relevant in our day: "Live simply so that others may simply live" and "Stewardship is everything we do with everything we have." A basic Anabaptist position is this: the joyful faithful are committed to a lifestyle which deemphasizes not only conspicuous consumption but buying and spending at any level which competes for the compassion dollar—the welfare of others which is in our hands (pocketbooks and bank accounts).

The final question of today's telephone calls is, "What shall we say?" How shall we respond? Two actual phone calls suggest how our conversation with God can have closure (for now). Jim, a young adult, called me one evening, saying that he was at the local bank. The loan officials were willing to take a lien on his car so that some additional funds could be made available for enlarging the coffeehouse ministry. Jim's assumption was obvious: the enlarged facility would permit a greater ministry. He wondered whether Thursday evening was a suitable night for them to come out and evaluate the coffeehouse.

I was glad that Jim couldn's see me shake my head or hear my thoughts. How unrealistic Jim was about everything: (1) how much money an enlargement requires, (2) what his old car was actually worth, (3) the ire that would be evoked in "touching" the old church, (4) how many committee meetings would come to pass before the trustees would see their way clear, (5) the difficulty of the board to decide on anything, and (6) whether an enlargement was the way to increase ministry. Jim interrupted my silence, "Well, what do you say?" And I heard myself saying, "Jim, that's beautiful."

Daughter Jan got a phone call for baby-sitting for a date on which there was a major family conflict. She told the caller, "Wait a minute," and then proceeded to get a variety of family perspectives. She returned to the mouthpiece and said quietly, "I think I can." Asked to repeat, she spoke firmly.

The calls come. Whenever we respond, even with the benefit of a variety of perspectives, even with the decision of giving up our chosen means of getting around or our special dates, and even though we will feel inadequate for the job, we will hear a response of God's Spirit bearing witness with ours. "That's beautiful, Jim/Jan. You got the message."

Sermon 2

God's Grace and Our Families

(John 4:7ff)

by LeRoy E. Kennel

A former 1st Lady of the U.S., Jackie Onassis, according to a current series of articles, dislikes being asked about her previous family life with Mr. O. She ignores questions about the pure gold plated faucets and the 42 telephones on his boat-house.

Do gold faucets and 42 phones make a happy home? The newspaper tells us daily of unhappy homes, homes broken by poverty of an economy or of mind and spirit.

Wherein do we find grace for our homelife, and when we do find it, to what do we attribute it? I overheard an acquaintance telling his friend about a new job with a church institution. His friend asked, "how did you get it?" The response was an exclamatory, "luck—I lucked out."

Our conference attempts to put one's finger on something more pure than gold faucets, to place hands on handles that open up something more telling than 42 extension phones, and that goes beyond Leo Buscaglia's "best-selling" book on LOVE, which stresses loving love and hugging strangers. This afternoon we evaluate whether or not the cause of newness and renewedness of family life is adequately stated in "luck—we lucked out."

Our biblical faith declares that in the midst of ordinary family life, we can live out our lives by God's Grace. John 4 is about God's grace which reaches out, first to a housewife who is a Samaritan, and then to a Gentile's sick son. These two incidents are the first admissions of Jesus of himself as the Messiah, the chosen instrument of grace. And the first story is one of grace given to a despised alien and aliented housewife.

The Samaritan woman story reminds us of the close parallels of individual conversion and of family change. It underscores how God's grace operates similarly in individual and group life. This story affirms a theme of this three day conference, that grace "happens" (lucks-in) not just with the perfect ones, the pure people, but with Samaritan housewives and Gentile children. God's grace is at work with ordinary family experiences, in less than perfect families. Shortly, Advent begins. Those worship leaders who will attempt to read publicly the "begats" of Matthew 1 and Luke 1 may bring some smiles to hearers as all of those names get pronounced in going from Adam to Jesus. But on second reading and third thoughts, we will be moved to tears, not amused, for that is a list of less than perfect families, including prostitutes and outsiders, all marching to Bethlehem for the birth of His Grace, Jesus, Savior of the world. John 4 is a story of such an unlikely example of the ideal housewife and homemaker, a long way from being a Princess Jacqueline, of royal blood.

Six premises emerge; six conclusions of God's grace and our families; six themes for further testing and fine-tuning in the lives of Illinois Mennonite homes and congregations; six testaments of God's desire for experiencing family life.

I. FAMILY GRACE COMES AS A GIFT. The great conviction of the Psalmites, of the writer John and of the preacher Paul, is that life itself is a gift, and so is one's desire to worship, one's impulse to believe, one's motivation to love, one's capacity to hope. This month's Thanksgiving time puts its finger on life's dynamic as that of gratitude, the ability to say "thank you." Babcock, in tracing thankfulness for bread keeps going back and back, from the loaf to the mill, to the grain, the shower, and ultimately to the Father's will. Paul's own conclusion is an exclamation of "eyes wide open to the mercies of God" to present himself as a living sacrifice in service to Christ and the church. John 4 identifies appreciation for family heritage and family chiefs, such as Jacob, after whom the well is named. Jacob, too, is a "given," a grace gift.

Marriage and family are gifts. The magnetic power is not something that one earns or does. It is something that comes as an initiative from another. It is something that wells up within oneself because of an outside attraction and presence. It is personally given and personally received. It is not something one decides for someone else or something that comes by mere intellectual decision or willful calculation. One name for it is grace. Blest be the tie of grace that binds and bonds our hearts in marriage and family.

It is Jesus who strikes up the conversation with the Samaritan woman, and not the other way around. She loves because he first loved her. Jesus had his eye on her before she had her eye on him. God so loved the world that God gave that special Son. It's amazing—grace.

Life, and life's responses, for people of biblical faith, is not one of lucking out but of looking out to what manner of love the Father has bestowed upon us that we should be called children of God and joint heirs with Jesus Christ.

II. FAMILY GRACE COMES IN THE ORDINARY WAY. Real drama is the extraordinary coming in the ordinary. Ordinarily, grace breaks into the family in ordinary times. And so it is that while the Samaritan woman is about her chores, while it is that she is working with that "list" of 100 details: dinner, drinks, shopping. It is with that list, our list, that she and we have experiences extraordinary.

The ordinary gives Jesus, too, the occasion for sharing grace. It is with a rest stop, where and when his disciples pause for refreshment. It is in the midday heat at a village near Sychar, the modern Askar, that Jesus asks this anonymous housewife for a drink of H_2O. Shortly, Jesus will make his famous words on "living water" as the metaphor of salvation (picking up on the lament of broken cisterns and stale waters of Jeremiah 2:13). Shortly he will discuss the relationship of this Mt. Gerazim overhere and that Mt. Zion overthere as to appropriateness for worship locations. Shortly he will discuss with his disciples about the crops and their bounty as the illustration of another kind of harvest. In a previous discussion he compared the Holy Spirit's movements with those of ordinary winds.

Grace is here and there—right in the routine and ordinary. We could find it right in our own families. An examination of my roots has a young man, age nineteen leaving Nancy, France by himself, coming to Ontario, Canada to work and then to Nebraska to farm. There my grandfather met Katie Zehr Roth who was born at Flanagan, IL, just twenty five miles East of here (She was the only grandparent I met. I recall the last time I saw her was when I was five. Dad had asked me to come into her bedroom where he and I sang "And when the battle's over we shall wear a crown." I saw Dad and his brothers in tears). "Family grace in the ordinary" occurred in the life of another nineteen year old person, my mother, Anna Reeb who was born near Low Point, IL, just five miles North of here. After confirmation at the Washburn Lutheran Church she moved at 19 to Nebraska where she met Dad. Many years later as he approached her hospital bed he overhears her saying to herself or was it God, "Jesus suffered, I can, too." Family grace in the ordinary occurred at the Evanston, IL Mennonite Church, after a sermon, teenage son Jon is assisting me with an antiphonal prayer with Jon giving one line of the hymn "Take My Life and Let It Be" after respective petitions that I gave. Unsolicited, grautitous offerings were made by a 3-year-old sibling Jay. After each of the eight statements from the "Take My Life" hymn by Jon, Jay gave his uninhibited, unplanned offering of "Amen." I love to tell that story: "family grace — in the ordinary."

   III. FAMILY GRACE COMES AS A PROCESS. One of our wise sayings, particularly in times of impatience, is "Rome was not built overnight." We can say that family grace comes in specific times and places; it comes from France to Tavistock at the age of 19 and moves from Lowpoint to Nebraska at 19, as well as happens in Evanston in a worship service. We can say also that it comes over time, particularly in developing and ongoing relationships. John 4 so illustrates:

   A. The Samaritan housewife sees more of grace in progressive increments.
   • "How is it that you being a Jew, ask water?"
   • "You say that you could give me a drink, without any equipment?"
   • "Are you greater than Jacob, our family chief, who had skills of watering umpteen livestock and people?"
   • "Can you give me such water so that I am satisfied, as well as helping me in chores?"
   • "Ah, I perceive (contemplate, such as in progressive insights) you are a prophet."
   • "Could this be the Messiah?"

As the woman sees more of Jesus, she in turn sees more of herself. As she grows in self discovery, she in turn sees more of Jesus. And her own reordering occurs in light of on-going relationships. It isn't forced, of course, but it comes — as grace in a relationship process!

   B. This premise and principle of family grace coming as a process is seen also in the way the disciples respond to Jesus. The scene is one of their marveling. First, they were surprised that he must needs go through Samaria. And now he was talking with a Samaritan, and a woman at that, and, moreover, he was asking something of her. Was he using this for a teaching opportunity, or what? They didn't ask: they were biting their tongues and biding his time.

   C. This premise of process also characterizes the townspeople, the extended family of the housewife. They weighed what she had said. Then they besought Jesus and requested his staying with them. After all of this, they themselves "saw."

   D. Jesus in all of these conversations and relationships uses the process. He permits the woman to come to her conclusions and insights through dialog and polite confrontation. He talks of the harvest with the disciples, using sayings of the day to illustrate how full of hope the situation was. He consents to stay for two days with the townspeople.

   Grace is in staying. As in Paul's conversion, he must spend three years in Arabia after his blinding love for the unfolding realization of the meaning of grace. Family grace too is a choice to stay — in a life-time pilgrimage. It is a way of life and of life commitment. The focus is not just on self but the other and on "our life together." Life-long commitment, and a series of choices, is the means, product, and event of Grace.

   Grace is in staying. "Rome isn't built overnight." It doesn't occur at the snap of a finger, but the "time is coming." How does one see the whole picture of grace but over time? If we were to each draw on a piece of paper — now, in our mind's eye — the floor plan of one of the floors of the house in which we lived at the age of 7, or the layout of one room, and then take our neighbor on a tour, and they in turn take us on one through theirs, it would help to illustrate the insight that comes through time. If I were to take you on a tour of my floor plan, I would show you Dad studying for his sermons at the kitchen table. Then I would take you to the bathroom, and note the free standing tub, under which on the East side is a wooden wagon with 26 wooden blocks with faded lettering—hand me downs from five older children. One rear wheel, the left side, has its rubber tread partly gone, as if cut off with a knife. The wagon bumps as it is pulled out, but the blocks are snugly packed and won't wiggle out. In the wagon is a can of marbles and I am playing with them during family devotions. Dad's hand is now on mine during his prayer. It doesn't pinch or squeeze too hard, just firmly yet gently holds. My story is now told with more maturity than at 7, or at 17. It is told with less distortion than last year and with more honesty. Family grace comes over time and with process.

IV. FAMILY GRACE COMES IN RECOGNITION OF BEING A LOVED SINNER. Sometimes we don't stay—for two days or two decades. We do leave home. We do become aliens and alienated. We do get separations and divorces. Then what?

When the woman at the well was thinking about the possibility of getting living water for her own thirst, she not only got in touch with her own requirements but also her own responsibilities. As if reading her mind about her family tasks, Jesus asked about her husband. Apparently, he wanted to offer him such water too. After the interchange on who and if there is a husband, she is most self conscious. But Jesus doesn't poke around in her past or try to argue whether or not the Mosaic rules and regulations had allowed her to have the status that she had. He is concerned about a new future. He explores with her new options for the present.

Marriage and family, as in conversion, concerns an embrace of holy life now. There is a radical resolute consciousness of a unique "adoption" into a family. There is preoccupation on one's options for the present and not on one's opting out of the past.

The *means* of grace comes in recognition of being a loved sinner. *A Raisin in the Sun* by Lorraine Hansberry has a scene that states that those who are treated as loved sinners in the present, that they will cope best with their past and respond most productively in the future. Son Walter has blown most of his Dad's life insurance policy and suggests to his mother how they might get back by mischievous ways a part of it which was a down payment on a house in a white neighborhood.

Beneatha: That is not a man. That is nothing but a toothless rat.

Mama: Yes—death done come in this here house. Done come walking in my house. On the lips of my children. You what supposed to be my beginning again. You—what supposed to be my harvest. You—you mourning your brother?

Beneatha: He's no brother of mine.

Mama: What you say?

Beneatha: I said that the individual in that room is no brother of mine.

Mama: That's what I thought you said. You feeling like you better than he is today? Yes? What you tell him a minute ago? That he wasn't a man? Yes? You give him up for me? You done wrote his epitaph too—like the rest of the world? Well, who give you the privilege?

Beneatha: Be on my side for once! You saw what he just did, Mama! You saw him—down on his knees. Wasn't it you who taught me—to despise any man who would do that? Do what he's going to do?

Mama: Yes—I taught you that. Me and your daddy. But I thought I taught you something else too . . . I thought I taught you to love him.

Beneatha: Love him? There is nothing left to love.

Mama: There is always something left to love. And if you ain't learned that, you ain't learned nothing. Have you cried for that boy today? I don't mean for yourself and for the family 'cause we lost the money. I mean for him; what he been through and what it done to him. Child, when do you think is the time to love somebody the most; when they done good and made things easy for everybody? Well then, you ain't through learning—because that ain't the time at all. It's when he's at his lowest and can't believe in hiself 'cause the world done whipped him so. When you starts measuring somebody, measure him right, child, measure him right. Make sure you done taken into account what hills and valleys he come through before he got wherever he is.

The approach recommended by Mama is also that used in John 8, when a family member is found in adultery. Jesus ministers to her not by condemning her, but commending acceptance and grace.

Precious memories, how they linger, but so do not-so-precious memories. Shall we forget them? Indeed, can we, let alone "should"? The good news is that God's grace comes to families and offers living water, not stale statements being juggled out of our mouths or jostled out of our cisterns of answerbooks. Former Senator Hughes of Iowa was speaking at Harrisonburg, VA. He was about to be served dessert before his speaking. The waitress must have said to herself, What if I were to spill this lemon chiffon pie on him—because that's exactly what she did. She rushed out and brought in towels, her face red with embarrassment. Senator Hughes offered her living water; he reached out and took her face in his hands and gave her a kiss. What would have been lingering nonprecious memories that night, what would have been too embarrassing to tell to family or friends, now could be told. It could be remembered IN NEW WAYS. When you are treated as a loved sinner, you are treated gracefully.

V. FAMILY GRACE COMES IN BEING LOVING SERVANTS. When the woman returned to the village, she told her extended family, her neighbors, her coworkers, her colleagues, all that she had experienced. Kissed with grace, experiencing being a loved sinner, she became a loving servant. Unselfconsciousness occurs when a family moves from the state of being burdened down to being liberated. The new discovery must be shared. Its a vocational mission, a sharing of mighty acts of grace. So the woman dashes to town. She draws others into her own house-church. She draws them into relation with Jesus. She represents Jesus.

Those who undergo family grace therapy will be inclined to reach out and draw others into that grace. A graced nuclear family explodes into an extended family. Family life continues to be a supreme conductor of Christianity. "We will know you are Christians by your love . . . by the way you guard each one's dignity, serve each one's pride, yes we know."

Dare we ask, Why we have not experienced more growth in our larger families, our congregations and conference? Lack of grace in our families? Minimum realization of being loved sinners? Unawareness of the possibilities of being loving servants? In Timothy's life, Paul recognized that the ministry was praiseworthy not just because of Timothy's work, but that of his mother Eunice and his grandmother Lois.

Servanting is not to be interpreted, therefore, as only valid when it is being exercised with other family units. A healthy family knows how to talk and how to listen with itself. Dolores Curran in *Traits of a Healthy Family,* for which she polled 500 professionals who work regularly with families, found that from fifteen qualities, communication was most often cited as central to close family life.

Speaking and listening communication is a family grace. Loving servants communicate. They paraphrase, "Are you saying that. . . . " They lay upon one another the dignity, "I hear you. . . . " Like the people of John 4, they ask questions; they ponder, they reflect, they marvel, talk with the disenfranchised, bite their tongues and bide someone's time.

They forgive in ways unlike the person who on his death bed called in another member of the family feud. He requested forgiveness and they shook hands. As the second party was leaving, the first said, "If I get over this and out of here, just remember the feud is still on."

Illinois Conference has featured a weekend program designed to be a family experience where all ages have an opportunity to speak and listen to each other regarding family life. Throughout, the planning committee dared believe that we may more clearly see God's grace operating in our families just as we experience them—warts and all, struggles and all. As loving servants it can be done.

VI. FAMILY GRACE COMES MOST AND BEST WHEN ONE IS IN A GODSPELL. The *Godspell* musical has a strange family emerging, strange in that they are a motly group, most heterogenious, and yet they are homogenius. Why? They have Christ in common. They are under the spell of Christ. They have been commonly graced. And they want to know Christ and to know Christ more fully, in the words of a lyric: "day by day, Oh Dear Lord, three things I pray: 1) to see thee more clearly, 2) to love thee more dearly, 3) to follow thee more nearly; as day by day . . . by day."

John 4:14 says that, indeed, there is a fountain filled with grace, one from which the family gets transfusion and from which it is transformed. It is divine energy: a gift of life from God, leaping up within us, fulfilling us and God's family plan. Jesus promises living/running water. The Old Testament writers used the term to describe God's action in restoring life: For my people have committed two evils: they have forsaken me, the fountain of living waters, and hewed out cisterns for themselves, broken cisterns, that can hold no water." Jeremiah 2:13.

For John and the early church community of faith, the real source of living water is found in Jesus Christ. John also understood the water of life (7:28) to be a designation for the Holy Spirit which purifies and quickens new life in us, that bestowed upon all who are ready and receptive.

One of the questions of the housewife was, where to worship. Jesus' reply was that the real question for being graced is not *where* but *how.* Valid gracing is not established by impressive pageantry in official santuaries (or on house-boats with gold plated faucets and 42 extensions), neither in the meeting house here at Metamora or at Science Ridge (if we so insist, that Zion-Gerizim problem is merely relocated). Nor is it in magical rites (I have here in this bottle entitled "Jacob's Well" water purchased there this April: shall we break the seal and all be touched with that water?). Special drinks, even the communion cup, cannot guarantee it.

One of the hopeful features of this conference is the realization that we who are graced with life and family, graced in our ordinary and over time, graced as loved sinners and as loving servants, can remain under that spell. This conference dares to claim that we who are privileged and called to honor God's name in shopping centers of the world as well as the sanctuaries of the church, that we can be honored by that name and honor that name in the family. What we now claim, let us also proclaim.

VII. THE STORY SEQUENCES

Thesis 7: A Sermon Is Effective When It Is in an Appropriate Worship Setting

No sermon is an island unto itself. It is part of a context, a continuum, a process in which each sharing of the story deepens and expands the implications of the previous telling, and prepares the way for the next telling. What beautiful patterns can emerge in these various sequences! Look carefully at the short and the long, the beginning and the end, the coming and the going, God and us!

Short Story—Long Story

Almost all human endeavors can be understood in terms of such a systems approach, recognizing the whole and not merely the part. Preachers will be frustrated and "throw in the towel" if they attempt to build their Rome on one days' sermon-story. Preaching as defined here has to do with finding faith-truth, and with making that discovery in some faith-context. The sermon research advocated in preceding chapters, for example, affirmed the Bible as the *essential base,* provided that it wasn't viewed as a static or propositional base. The sermon research advocated here calls for a "longer" search through an additional faith-context in hopes of finding the faith-truth there as well. Past storytellers and forms of stories—such as carols, creeds, confessions, case studies, characters, and commentaries—were suggested as part of that larger repertoire of story resources. A third part of the longer search is dialog with the present faith-context; there, too, one can find faith-truth. The coalescing of these three aspects of sermon research has been recommended as that adequate vertical exegesis for preaching and telling it like it is.

This dynamic course of sermon research has its counterpart in the preacher's dynamic resource. "The preacher, whose mind has been excited by the biblical writings" seeks to transmit that excitation into the minds of the hearers.[1] The sermon, therefore, is a present revelation of faith-truth through a convinced witness/storyteller who shares with other storytellers (the congregation), who in turn re-enter the world as the living, witnessing presence of that story.

Just as the message inherent in the story we share was not finished by the biblical writers, nor by some-place or some-one or some specific time in heritage or history, neither will it be finished by the preacher and congregation *today.* Those kairos-units that make up our sharing of the story are too short to tell the whole story. The purpose of a given sermon-story is to create the possibility of new revelation.

The sermon-story hermeneutic is both artistic-evocative and community-public. It is artistic-evocative because the preacher is not primarily trying to defend or prove, not trying to shore up some static argument, but to "render" faith-reality in its fullness and by the act of storytelling to "lure" hearers.[2] The preacher's hope is not so much to win acceptance as it is to stimulate inner revelation on the hearer's own part, to unfold the petals of the bud of faith. The hermeneutic is community-public because it is not merely the needs and situation of the immediate occasion that are at stake, but the lessons of the original "revelation", the heritage of subsequent history, and the implications of tomorrow. The sermon-story builds upon each new weeks' sharing, and takes its energy from the response of all storytellers, preacher, and congregation.

The act of preaching also carries beyond the moment in that it extends to concerns beyond the context of a given service. It will lead to counseling; it will lead to conflict; it will confront the fullness of life and experience, and not be trapped behind stained-glass windows and arched doors. Faith cometh by many hearings of many telling. Bachman reminds that "preaching might be defined as the artistic juxtaposing of past and present religious insights for the purpose of generating more of the same."[3] All of the short-kairos times, each telling and sharing of the story, contributes indispensably to the long-view.

Prelude—Postlude

A single worship service is a whole story—made of parts that work together. As is true of a symphony, there is a major theme which reoccurs, and there are secondary themes. At times, as in improvisational jazz, the music may go off in one direction; when it returns, some folk start clapping and many rejoice in "what was made of it". Each instrument (person and part) has a special function: all are needed, all have their unique sound. There is orchestration. The jazz conductor may walk to the side but things are in control and under discipline.

One simple possible set of experiences of worship (without the eucharist) is suggested in the following outline:

> The Community Gathers
> Prelude
> Call to Worship and Prayer of Readiness
>> The Community Responds to God's Love
> Hymn of Praise
> Prayer of Confession
> Declaration of Pardon
> Passing of Peace
>> The Community Receives God's Word
> Old Testament Lesson
> Responsorial Psalm or Hymn
> Epistle Lesson
> Gospel Lesson
> Sermon
>> The Community Responds to God's Word

Prayers of the People
Offerings of the People
Hymn of Dedication
Benediction
Postlude

One Lesson — One Lectionary

The "sample service" sequence above has more than one scripture reading. This is the recommendation of the lectionary, a guide designed to provide both a balanced teaching program of the biblical story as well as a comparative telling of the story within a three-year cycle. Weekly coverage includes an Old Testament reading, an epistle, a gospel, and an appropriate Psalm. The lectionary's coverage is like a well-planned menu. Why should one be satisfied then with only baked potatoes or roasting ears? Why only sparse and spartan diets when a little dessert is possible (fresh strawberries!)?

The lectionary also promises that we won't overlook an important element in the telling of the story as it indeed is.[4] Moreover, in its cycle plan, it puts us in touch with the larger story and gives us an opportunity to tell it again each year. The theme "Deny yourself" needs to be followed by the theme of "Rejoice, and again I say, Rejoice." We need the first half of the year, from Advent to Pentecost; but we also need the next half of the year to work out what these events mean in the life and acts of the congregation. When Christmas comes again, it is not the same story that is told again. The congregation, the preacher, the other liturgies, all have changed. And some aspects of the world have changed, too. The next year, the next cycle, is new. As in a spiral staircase, we have come back to touch the same vertical line, but we touch it at a higher place. We are climbing Jacob's ladder! Being "changed from glory to glory", it is proper indeed to retell our story—but *this* time with less distortion, with more honesty, with greater muturity.

A lectionary also provides enrichment and enlargement of a given thesis. The use of the lectionary is comparable to two or more persons counseling together. Its value is akin to getting advice from several doctors. It need not be a wooden, static, restrictive experience, preventing one from relying primarily on one of the readings, or substituting one of them, or even replacing the set altogether on a given day.

A lectionary's objective of several scriptures working together can be illustrated with the decision to preach on *shalom,* God's blessing of enabling peace for all people. Shalom's meaning includes two central thoughts: the heart of the Gospel is God's good gift of peace given *to* us and *through* us. It is peace in the heart after a night's struggle, when the Jacob within us is given a new name, and no longer are we the deceitful one but the anointed one (Genesis 32:22–30). It is peace given in the hour of death to Jesus after a short intense life of mission (John 14:27–19). It is in this context that Jesus makes out his will and we become recipients of that inheritance. This gift contains the opportunity, moreover, for new disposition in the midst of community struggles (Romans 12:17–21). Peace is given in the midst of the accidents and accents of life. Peace as work-witness is the excitement of realizing that peace is also given through us! It is to work for peace with one's brother Esau, after being given the gift of peace after the night of struggle. It is to go forth loving one's enemy, one's Judas, after a night of prayer in the Garden. It is to live in peace with the Romans even as they continue their armaments build-up and their worship of militarism. As agents and ambassadors of peace and reconciliation we are people who at worship hear afresh the Word of God in Jesus Christ, about the God of peace who unites to people in peace, and creates peace through people of peace.

The Sermon — The Eucharist

Liturgical preaching is part of a larger proclamation when it is undertaken in tandem with the Lord's Supper/Holy Communion/The Eucharist. These are parts of the same story. The one is a more visual and an acted-out counterpart. Both are sacramental, if by that word we can mean places of meetings, a sign of Christ being present with us. Both provide opportunity to "do this in remembrance" — to engage in living memory. When the sermon precedes the "great thankgiving" (eucharist) it can open the worshipper to receive Christ as power to live in the world. As complementary junctions for faith to be operative, they are liturgical storytelling constituents.

There are other special services that can be tied in tandem and counterpoint to the sermon. They, too, are sacramental signs and storytelling constituents. The footwashing service of John 13 is such a service, whether it be done literally or not, whether it be an approximation or an alteration, such as a service of washing hands. It is a sign of love humbling itself for mission.

Enter to Worship — Depart to Serve

If Mercea Iliade is correct that there is a sacramental value to almost everything, then myths and symbols of life and life rhythms are most important for telling the whole story. That story includes the rhythms of weekday and weekend, the witness of the congregation both when it worships and when it works, and the rituals when it gathers for worship and when it scatters for service. All have sacramental value, all interface, and all are interdependent. In that detailing, the rhythm of the local congregation will touch all bases: (1) who we are — clarification of identity; (2) where we are — defining the world situation; (3) what we are doing — engaging in self-study; (4) what God wants us to do — choosing actions; (5) how we are doing — evaluating; (6) how we rejoice — celebrating the actions of one through five. Each of these facets feeds into the others. None is optional. None is mutually exclusive or entirely inside or outside of the church's storytelling. What happens on the worship order "side" of the bulletin feeds into and back again from the "announcements side".

The journey inward must always be accompanied by the journey outward. Praying that God's will be done occurs also when we get off of our knees to become answers to the prayers. It occurs when we become instrumental in creating a world where peace and justice get attention and get action, when piety and practice stay married, when hospitality is exercised outside as well as inside.

The worship and service sequence is at the heart of liturgy. The work of the people is in "the temple and synagogue" where stories are told and it is in the courtyard and fields where vocations are lived out. Christ lived within and without, imitating and emulating, finding and following, assimilating and participating, these belong together in the story sequence. Both the praise of God and the service to people make up a coherent, consistent, and comprehensive Christian story.

God — Us

"God created man because he loves stories" was the way this project began. That is the way it continued, and we now can say that God recreates us through that love of stories. We asked in this declaration "who" is the story-lover — "God" or "man"? Is God's telling an act of vocation? Is our telling an exploration of our origin, identity, and relationship with God? By examining the method and ministry of preaching as shared story, we now know the answer is "all of the above". Even as we took our start, so now we take our stand with the thesis that God's relationship with people is at the heart of religious communication.

Seven theses of preaching can be summed up in one greater command: we shall love the Lord our God, the Author of stories. And the second is like unto it: we shall love the Lord our God, the Authorizer of stories — even, and especially, the shared story of preaching.

Notes

Chapter 1. The Story Idea

1. James B. Wiggins (ed.), *Religion as Story* (Harper & Row, 1975), p. ix. For additional insight into the function of story, see the special issue of *Theology Today,* Vol. 32, No. 2, July 1975, "Symposium on Narrative & Story in Theology".
2. Stephen Crites, "The Narrative Quality of Experience", *Journal of the American Academy of Religion,* Vol. XXXIX, No. 3, Sept. 1971, pp. 305–306.
3. Alfred Lord, *Singer of Tales* (Harvard University, 1970).
4. Frederick Buechner, *Telling the Truth: The Gospel as Tragedy, Comedy, & fairy Tale* (Harper & Row, 1977).
5. – – –, *The Sacred Journey* (Harper & Row, 1982).
6. Ibid.
7. See Sallie TeSelle, *Speaking in Parables — A Study in Metaphor and Theology* (Fortress Press, 1975), for an insightful elaboration.
8. Original draft given to the writer by Alan Kieffaber, and published in "From Preacher to Congregation", by LeRoy Kennel, *Brethren Life and Thought,* Winter, 1980, Volume XXV, p. 40.
9. B. F. Jackson (ed.), *Communication — Learning for Chruchmen* (Abingdon, 1968), pp. 81–82.
10. Reuel L. Howe, "Letter from the Director", Institute for Advanced Pastoral Studies Newsletter, Fall, 1971. David Buttrick's *Homiletic — Moves and Structures* (Fortress, 1987) defines preaching's function similarly, as that which does not persuade via arguing the truth of the gospel but as setting "the gospel in lived experience, genuine experience, so that truth will be acknowledged" p. 33. The point of such preaching (all preaching) is to teach congregations to interpret their experience in the light of scripture and the scripture in view of their experiences. Preaching, according to Buttrick, can change our identity by incorporating all our stories into God's story. Its aim, therefore, is to construct in consciousness a "faith-world" related to God. As story such preaching confers identity.
11. Joseph Sittler, *Anguish of Preaching* (Fortress Press, 1966), p. 7.

12. Good resources on story theory as applied to preaching and religious commuication are *Preaching the Story* by Steimle, Niedenthal & Rice (Forgress, 1980); *Preaching & Story* (Academy of Homiletics, 1979); *Caring Enough to Hear & Be Heard* by David Augsburger (Herald Press, 1982); Sunday after Sunday, *Preaching the Homily as Story* by Robert Waznak (Paulist Press, 1983).

13. Many story theorists develop the left side-right side of the brain relevance for sharing cognitive/affective materials. Robert Bela Wilhelm, pubisher of *Story Fest Quarterly* (San Francisco) shares this view.

Chapter II. The Story Book

1. Warren Groff, *Storytime: God's and Ours* (Bethany Press, 1974).

2. I am indebted to Gabriel Fackre, author of *Word in Deed* (Eerdman,s 1975), for this concept, which I have applied to preaching.

3. These "attitudes" and "actions" were developed by Richard Gardner of the Church of the Brethren Offices, Elgin, Illinois, and were shared in a team-taught preaching class, "Interpretation and Communication: Preaching" at Bethany Theological Seminary, Oak Brook, IL.

4. Ernest Best, *From Text to Sermon* (John Knox Press, 1978).

5. Leander Keck, *The Bible in the Pulpit* (Abingdon, 1978).

6. Willard M. Swartley, *Case Studies in Biblical Interpretation — Slavery, Sabbath, War and Women* (Herald Press, 1983), p. 190.

7. Ibid., pp.150–191.

8. James A. Sanders, *God Has a Story Too — Sermons in Context* (Fortress, 1979), p. 8. Sanders' further work, *From Sacred Story to Sacred Text* (Fortress, 1987), gives additional help to use the church's book — a task not reserved for isolated scholars but for persons involved directly in the life of the church who are struggling with issues of faith and obedience. The process of translating a biblical thought or event to today is the process discovered in the Bible itself, in the study of canonization, where God as "the Integrity of Reality" is at work shaping the community of faith, giving them identity and saving them from idolatries. "Careful, responsible, critcal study of the Bible in terms of its dialogue through the ages with those communities of faith that bequeathed it to us provides the paradigm for the same dialogue to continue among their heirs today" (p. 194).

9. Ibid., p. 23.

10. Ibid., p. 24.

11. A good discussion of Ricoeur is found in Lewis Mudge's *Paul Ricoeur — Essay on Biblical Interpretation* (Fortress, 1980). David Buttrick in his *Homiletic — Moves and Structures*, discusses "moves" as the power of words and syntax to bring into view "convictional understandings and Christian rhetoric as "bringing out and into view" through the means of metaphor. Thus, Christian rhetoric associates, putting together Christian understandings with images of lived experience. "The rhetoric of association is a language of imagery, illustration, example, testimony and the like" p. 42. Noting that preaching may be labeled "sacred rhetoric" Buttrick says it is clearly a poetic activity — invoking, bringing Presence to consciousness through telling of stories and exploring of images. The conclusion — "preaching is a work of metaphor" p. 113.

12. Robert D. Young, *Religious Imagination* (Westminster Press, 1979), p. 14.

13. Ibid., p. 48.
14. Ibid., p. 111.

Chapter III. The Story Resources

1. Robert M. Grant, "Apostles' Creed", in *Twentieth Century Encyclopedia of Religious Knowledge,* Volume 1 (Baker, 1965), p. 54.
2. Three examples of teaching and preaching based upon the Apostles' Creed include: O. Sydney Barr, *From the Apostles' Faith to the Apostles' Creed* (Oxford, 1964); William Barclay, *The Apostles' Creed for Everyman* (Harper & Row, 1967); James D. Smart, *The Creed in Christian Teaching* (Westminister, 1962).
3. Harold A. Bosley, *Preaching on Controversial Issues* (Harper, 1953), p. 23.
4. James Wm. McClendon, Jr., *Biography as Theology* (Abingdon, 1974), p. 203.
5. "Theology: The Storyteller's", *Newsweek,* December 31, 1973, p. 25.
6. "Any" life can serve as an encouragement, not just "believers". John Dunne's writings are in the form of "subtly nuances journeys through the great myths, stories, biographies, and autobiographies of world literature; his method is to simply help us pass over by sympathetic understanding" to other lives and epochs and to return with enriched insights in the spiritual adventure.
7. Stanley Hauerwas and David Burrell, "Self-Deception and Autobiography: Theological and Ethical Relfections on *Speer's Inside the Third Reich*", *The Journal of Religious Ethics,* Spring, 1974.
8. R. E. C. Browne's *The Ministry of the Word* (SCM Press, 1958) has an excellent discussion of how poetry is integral to effective preaching.
9. Unpublished paper by the author, "Worship as Experience", presented at Ministers' Conference, Mennonite Seminary, Fresno, CA, January, 1983.
10. Regis Duffy, *Real Presence* (Harper & Row, 1982), p. 59.
11. An example is *Introduction to Philosophy—A Case Study Approach* by Jack B. Roger and Forrest Baird (Harper & Row, 1981).
12. A case study is the nearest thing to actual experience. "It could have happened like this, Assume that it did." Often a case study does grow out of an actual life situation. Realistic imagination plus good writing did the rest.

    Careful preparation is also needed in study of the case study. The following steps are useful in preparing for a group interchange.
    A. Use realistic imagination to develop a clear mental picture of the situation.
    B. List the cast of characters.
    C. Develop a time limit of events in the case.
    D. Identify the basic issues about which decisions must be made.
    E. Emphathize: put yourself in the position of one or more individuals in the case to see how each would react.
    F. Think of any models or theory which might be helpful in clarifying the issue or resolving the problem in the case.

    The actual interchange among peers is as important as solitary study in the use of the case method. As a small group discuss the above steps, especially in listing the cast of characters and in indentifying the issues. Share points of view and insight. Ask what is the best solution? Take a vote. Role play.

The illustrative case study. "Gomer" is a creative poem of how the people of faith, including those who wrote scripture, and who have preached from it, have built up a concept that shows women as whores, as the "weaker vessel." Although this is a work of art, congruent with liberation theology, Is there a violation of proper interpretation of scripture? Is Hulda oblivious to the religious practices of Hosea's day which related religion and sex? Is Hulda seeing that males are whores also, and that unfaithfulness is a "when"? and what will Professor Webb do when Hulda asks him to assist her in chapel?

13. James Wm. McClendon, Jr. (Systematic Theology: Ethics (Abingdon Press, 1986), p. 356.
14. J. Randall Nichols, *Building the Word* (Harper & Row, 1980), pp. 140–141.
15. Examples include: Gordon C. Bennett's *Reader Theater Comes to Church* (John Knox Press, 1972); Michael Moynahan's *How the Word Became Flesh: Story Dramas for Worship and Religious Education* (Resource Publications, 1981); W. A. Poovey's *Mustard Seeds and Wine Skins* (Augsburg, 1972).
16. Adapted from the author's "Film as Storyteller — Augmenting Myth through Verbal and Visual Icons in 'On the Waterfront' ", *Mythos Papers,* 1983.
17. Frank McConnell, *Storytelling & Mythmaking* (Oxford, 1979).

Chapter IV. The Story Lands

1. Alfred Edyvean, *This Dramatic World* (Friendship Press, 1970).
2. J. B. Phillips, *Your God Is Too Small* (Macmillan, 1957).
3. *Chicago Daily News,* Good Friday, April, 1968.
4. *Markings,* translated by Leif Sjobert and W. H. Auden (Alfred A. Knopf, Inc., 1965).
5. Carl Michalson, "Communicating the Gospel", *Motive,* March 1957, p. 5.
6. Wayne Oates, *The Christian Pastor* (Westminister.)
7. Caroll A. Wise's *Pastoral Counseling* (Harper & Row, 1951), affirms the group-individual ministry: "Whether the pastor is dealing with a group or with an individual, he should be trying to reach the individual person. The approach and technique may be different, the goal the same. The fact is that some human needs may be met only in group relationships, while other needs may be met only in a close person-to-person relationship such as offered in counseling. The pastor who maintains the awareness that the essence of a religious ministry is to persons will see the individual group approaches as different aspects of a central function."
8. Charles F. Kemp, *Pastoral Preaching* (The Bethany Press, 1963), p. 12.
9. – – –, *Life-Situation Preaching* (The Bethany Press, 1956), p. 15.
10. Harry Emerson Fosdick, "What Is the Matter with Preaching?", *Harper's,* Volume 157, July, 1928. Fosdick's theory on pastoral preaching is as follows: "Every sermon should have for its main business the solving of some problem — a vital, important problem, puzzling minds, burdening consciences, distracting lives. . . . This endeavor to help people solve their spiritual problems is a sermon's only justifiable aim. The point of departure and of constant reference, the reason for preaching the sermon in the first place and the inspiration for its method of approach and the organization of its material should not be something outside the congregation but inside. . . . Any preacher who even with moderate skill is thus helping folk to solve their real problems." In similar concern, Howard Clinebell offers fifteen tests for preaching to accomplish pastoral preaching, which to him is the helping word for mental and spiritual health:

(1) Does preaching build bridges or barriers between people?

(2) Does preaching strengthen or weaken a basic sense of trust and relatedness to the universe?

(3) Does preaching stimulate or hamper the growth of inner freedom and personal responsibility? Does it encourage healthy or unhealthy dependency relationships—mature or immature relationships with authority? Does it encourage growth of mature or immature consciences?

(4) Does preaching provide effective or faulty means of helping persons move from a sense of guilt to forgiveness? Does it provide well-defined, significant, ethical guidelines, or does it emphasize ethical trivia? Is its primary concern for surface or for the underlying health of the personality?

(5) Does preaching increase or lessen the enjoyment of life? Does it encourage a person to appreciate or depreciate the feeling dimension of life?

(6) Does preaching handle the vital energies of sex and aggressiveness in constructive or repressive ways?

(7) Does preaching encourage the acceptance or denial of reality? Does it foster magical or mature religious beliefs? Does it encourage intellectual honesty with respect to doubts? Does it oversimplify the human situation or face its tangled complexity?

(8) Does preaching emphasize love and growth or fear?

(9) Does preaching give its adherents a "frame or orientation and object of devotion" that is adequate in handling existential anxiety constructively?

(10) Does preaching encourage the individual to relate to the riches of his or her unconscious through living symbols?

(11) Does preaching accommodate itself to the neurotic patterns of the society or endeavor to change them? Does it challenge and change the instiutional structures of oppression?

(12) Does preaching strengthen or weaken self-esteem?

(13) Does preaching encourage sexism or androgyny (psychic wholeness)?

(14) Does preaching help to create responsible social as well as individual consciences in persons? Does it encourage ecological (whole-planet) awareness, caring, and response-ability?

(15) Does preaching facilitate the full development of the riches of the potentialities of people—the flowering of the full gifts of God in each individual?

Howard J. Clinebell, Jr., *The Mental Health Ministry of the Local Church* (Abingdon Press, 1972).

11. Donald Capps, *Pastoral Counseling and Preaching—A Quest for an Integrated Ministry* (Westminster, 1980).

12. Merrill R. Abbey, *Preaching to the Contemporary Mind* (Abingdon Press, 1963), p. 67.

13. Ibid., p. 72.

14. Arthur Van Seters, "Preaching as Revolutionary Witness—Opting for Social Hermeneutics", Unpublished Working Document for Academy of Homiletics.

15. Paul Scherer, *The Word God Sent* (Harper & Row, 1965), pp. 23–24.

16. "The Preaching Situation: Generic and Contextual Considerations", presented at the Speech Communication Convention, Chicago, December 28, 1974.

17. Bosley, p. 16f.

18. Merrill R. Abbey, *Living Doctrine in a Vital Pulpit* (Abingdon, 1964), p. 7.

19. Fred Craddock, *Overhearing the Gospel* (Abingdon, 1978).
20. Belden C. Lane, *Story Telling: The Enchantment of Theology* (The Bethany Press, 1982); also see John Harrell, "Teacher as Storyteller", *Baptist Leader,* Sept. 1978.
21. Stanley Hauerwas, *Truthfulness and Tragedy: Further Investigations into Christian Ethics* (University of Notre Dame Press, 1977).
22. Ralph E. Knupp's paper, "The Apologetic Preaching of Paul Tillich", presented at the Speech Communication Convention, Chicago, December 28, 1974.
23. Hauerwas, *Truthfulness and Tragedy.*
24. George Gerbner, "Television", *The Cresset,* p. 24.
25. Donald N. Oberdorfer, *Electronic Christianity: Myth or Ministry* (Brekke, 1982).

Chapter V. The Story Forms

1. Milton Crum, Jr., *Manual on Preaching* (Judson Press, 1977).
2. Eugene Lowry, *The Homiletical Bind* (John Knox Press, 1980).
3. H. Grady David, *The Design of the Sermon* (Muhlenberg Press, 1958).
   A discussion of Davis' theory together with an illustrated sermon is found in the author's unpublished dissertation, *Communication Constructs in Contemporary American Protestant Preaching* (Michigan State University, 1966).
4. Seymour Chatman, *Story and Discourse* (Cornell University Press, 1978) pp. 9–16.
5. See Richard Thulin's "Preaching and Narrative: A Bibliography" (*Religious Communication Today—The Journal of the Religious Speech Communication Association,* September, 1986). Two excellent resources are Robert Alter's *The Art of Biblical Narrative* (Basic Books, 1981) which uses the literary binoculars on the Old Testament of the four rubrics of words, actions, dialogue and narration, and James Wm. McClendon, Jr.'s *Ethics* (Abingdon, 1986) which applies narrative theory to theology and ethics, using the constructs of plot, character and setting.
6. Richard Jensen, *Telling the Story,* pp. 151–160.
7. Jensen further recommends, at least for "beginners" with the story format, that parallels of the biblical text be created. The point is to recast the parable in the language and people of the congregation's own world. He commends judicious use of silence. He stresses meditations on biblical texts with the backdrop of stories from literature, theater, cinema, television, music, and human life.
8. Martin Buber, *I and Thou* (Scribners, 1970) Trs. by Walter Kaufmann; also *Between Man & Man* (Macmillan, 1960).
9. *Between Man and Man,* p. 19.
10. Raymond E. Anderson, unpublished paper on "Martin Buber's Philosophy of Dialogue".
11. Adaptations are multiple, especially with choral readings. Fourteen persons may be used to tell "This Is Our Ministry" or it may be told by seven people with each one doubling (Oscar Rumpf, *Cries from the Hurting Edges of the World,* John Know Press, 1970); *"Sorry the Rice Is Gone"* (same collection) is designed for many voices but can be told by two persons. "The Dragon" in Gordon C. Bennett's *Happy Tales, Fables, and Plays* (John Knox, 1975), see also his *Reader's Theater Comes to Church,* is a fable which can be told by one, two, or three persons.
12. An example is William D. Thompson and Gordon C. Bennett's *Dialogue Preaching* (Judson Press, 1969).

13. James A. Sanders, *God Has a Story Too—Sermons in Context* (Fortress, 1979).
14. Myron Bloy (ed.), *Multi-Media Worship, A Model and Nine Viewpoints* (Seabury, 1979).

Chapter VI. The Storytellers

1. Marvin A. Gardner, Jr., "The Word Within", *College of Preachers Newsletter,* Fall, 1973.
2. The point of "a living center" is one of the distinguishing features of the nature of stories discussed by Richard Hensen in his *Telling the Story* (Augsburg, 1980), p. 114f.
3. James Barber as quoted in *Time,* September 12, 1969, p. 58.
4. James A. Forbes, "The Holy Spirit and the Preacher", *College of Preachers Newsletter,* Summer, 1979.
5. Kyle Haselden, *The University of Preaching* (Harper & Row, 1963).
6. James Cone, "The Story Context of Black Theology," *Theology Today,* Symposium on Narrative and Story in Theology, July, 1975, p. 129f.
7. Henry H. Mitchell, *Black Preaching,* (Lippincott, 1970).
8. Bryant Kirkland, "Expository Preaching Revitalized", *Pulpit Digest,* July-August, 1965.
9. F. Thomas Trotter, "Preaching and the Uses of Imagination", given at the Western Association of homilectics Professors, Claremont, CA, February, 1970.
10. An illuminating discussion of caring filled with memorable statements by Milton Mayoff, *On Caring* (Perennial Library, Harper & Row, 1971).
11. Charles Truax and Robert Carkhuff, *Toward Effective Counseling and Psychotherapy* (Aldine Publishing Co., 1967).
12. Hans Van Der Geest, *Presence in the Pulpit* (John Know Press, 1981), claims perceived credibility is affected by the overuse of "I". When the preachers says "I", it is not necessarily an egotistical accounting. When "I" is spontaneously spoken, it can be an expression of an agreement that "reigns between visible and audible behavior and inner attitude". It can express both an understanding of what is needed and that the preacher stands behind what is said, a standing of the whole person—including enthusiasm and seriousness.
13. Edgar Jackson, *How to Preach to People's Needs* (Abingdon, 1956), p. 13.
14. Paulo Friere, *Pedagogy of the Oppressed* (Continuum, 1981).
15. These lectures are contained in two books: *Jesus Came Preaching* (Scribners, 1931) and *Christ and History* (Abingdon, 1963).
16. Marvin J. Dirks, *Laymen Look at Preaching* (Christopher Publishing House, 1972).
17. One example is William D. Thompson's *A Listener's Guide to Preaching* (Abingdon, 1966).
18. Adapted from the author's "Developing Spirituality through a Group Approach to Free Church Liturgy", a paper presented at the North American Academy of Liturgy, Washington, D.C., 1979.
19. J. D. Glick, "Confessional Preaching", *The Christian Ministry,* Sept. 1977, p. 25f.

Chapter VII. The Story Sequences

1. J. Victor Bachman, "The Essential Base", an unpublished paper.
2. Process theology's concern for "lure" as indirect persuasion has high congruence with that of storytelling.

3. Bachman, "The Essential Base".
4. See William Willimon's *Intergrative Preaching* (Abingdon, 1981); *Preaching and Worship* (Academy of Homiletics, 1980) LeRoy E. Kennel (ed.); "Liturgical Preaching—a Neglected Child", presented by LeRoy E. Kennel, Academy of Homiletics, Toronto, 1983; also *Social Themes of the Christian Year* by Deter T. Hessel (ed.) (Geneva Press, 1983).

Appendix 1

The Ministry of Communication

Communication is ministry used powerfully when it is a means of greater awareness, when it helps to remove one's own masks, when it assists in declaring oneself. Particularly instructive is Jesus' use of the parable: descriptive common experiences that challenge the hearer to come up with the answer, to arrive at one's own conclusion, to see the truth for oneself, to make the insight one's own. The first mark of meaningful ministry is that communication be a translator of experience.

We discover communication at its best in Luke 24 where it is a generative experience for those Emmaus men. While on the move, there is a pointing to one in their midst who is identified as belonging to them. In this talking they discover who and whose they are, and as they find each other they are also able to celebrate more of their wholeness. It is this pointing and remembering talk that translates as well as generates experience. In the ministry of communication it is therefore important to probe the central questions that concern the meaning of human experience and then relate how Jesus is the one in whom we see the truth about our experiences.

A second aspect of interpersonal speech communication is that it is *enabling*. Jesus begins the Luke 24 dialogue by listening. He asks a simple question about current events, and then attempts to place those events in the context of the human pilgrimage. As a result the Emmaus men are enabled to discover themselves in meaningful and motivated responsibility. So it has always been God's purpose in the communicating ministry to establish a loving community in which humankind is made free to grasp the opportunity to love and serve one another. Accordingly, communicators are prompted to introduce not a forgotten God, but to indicate the presence of a living God of change who makes all things new.

Servanthood is a third term that characterizes a meaningful style of ministry. Jesus served others by explicating their situation. Some he afflicted, some he comforted; for all he clarified. The highest good for others is the servant role of explicating. Unfortunately, Christian communication is too often compliant—that is, it serves some fixated or arrested outlook or view, some easy answer or solution which fails to minister, to serve openness and authentic freedom. It fails to behold causal relations, new perceptions, and options. The consequence of and sequel to this failure is a decreased tolerance for ambiguity, uncertainty, ambivalence, and tension. . . . Jesus "opened to us the scriptures." The result is that the men are both infused with new life and with responsible use of power. Their ways of life was crucified. Robbed of the demonic power of fear, they went forth using the power of communication as servants again.

From THE CHRISTIAN MINISTRY by LeRoy Kennel, published by the Christian Century Foundation, January 1972.

Another aspect of this communication ministry is its use of contextual or firsthand *situational* materials. The raw materials are the things and persons about which one must exercise choice. Then the Bible is brought to these human experiences. A communicating ministry does not occur in retreat from reality. Rather, it deals with actual needs of those uprooted, bewildered, and betrayed. This use of first-hand materials is the best way to avoid a false pietism or unreal biblicism. On broken sidewalks we find Jesus walking; in today's burning bushes we find God speaking, and from those we communicate good news. The model is that of Jesus using a current event: "What is this conversation you are holding with each other as you walk?"

A fifth communicating guideline for ministry is that of *utilizing* the various media. When Jesus partially failed with words he used visual acts in the common secular act of breaking bread. When he employed both eye and ear methods, people were able to recognize and experience communication. It was Jesus who demonstrated that communication must shift from mere lecture to creating an environment for self-discovery. Communication is now a synthesis of many arts.

Appendix 2

An assignment in "Minister as Communicator" class as fulfilled by these four students can contribute to an understanding of a theology of preaching.

Communication Credo—Wilda W. (Wendy) Morris

What are we,
     man/woman/child,
         that God is mindful of us,
    the children of man/woman
        that God communicates with us?
For God made us little less than the angels,
     made us in the image of God
        in the image of the creating God,
           the Divine Communicator,
           the One whose Word was made flesh
              and tented among us,
              full of grace and truth
                truth, key to authentic communication
          the image of Truth,
           made flesh and tenting/living/dwelling
           among us.
We were made in God's image,
     in order that God's word might take root in our understanding
     in order to communicate to us
        communicate with us
           God's love,
           God's justice,
           God's righteousness,
           God's salvation,
           the joys and demands of God's Kingdom
        communicate with us
           relationship.
God made us that we might image
        God's love
        God's justice
        God's righteousness,
        God's salvation,
        the joys and demands of God's Kingdom,
    communicating the Word

the message of the Divine Communicator
to man/woman/child
made in the image of God.
We were made that we might enflesh God's Word,
the Truth
truth, key to authentic communication
that we might also enflesh our words
enflesh them in action,
in gesture,
in body language
enflesh them in relationship
and dwell with integrity,
authentically,
communicatingly,
among man/woman/child
made in the image of God;
that having enfleshed God's Word
we might reveal new meanings for a new age,
interpret the old stories,
poems,
prophecies,
proverbs
for our generation,
create a new community of communication
on which can be built the Kingdom of God.
God has made us little less than the angels,
made us in the image of the listening God,
the One who heard the cry of God's people in Egypt,
of God's people in exile,
heard the petition of the people
and their praise,
heard their distress and their joy;
the One who hears the cry of God's people today,
in Chicago,
in Moscow,
in El Salvador,
in Iran,
who hears the cry of God's people,
suffering,
celebrating,
questioning,
wondering,
learning,
hesitating,
growing.

We were made in the image of the listening God
that we might listen
        as God listens;
that we might hear the cry of God's people,
        of God's people today,
        in Chicago,
        in Moscow,
        in El Salvador,
        in Iran;
of God's people in our own homes,
            neighborhood,
            offices,
            classes,
            churches;
God's people suffering,
        celebrating,
        questioning,
        wondering,
        learning,
        hesitating,
        growing,
and that we, made in the image of God,
        might help man/woman/child
            to whom we listen,
            with whom we tent/live/dwell
                to image the creating God
                the listening God,
                the communicating God,
                    the God whose Word dwells among us as Truth—
                        truth, key to authentic communication.
We were made in God's image
        that in communicating with man/woman/child
            we might communicate with God, the Divine Communicator.

Communication Credo — Deanna Brown

A Friday evening concert, Orchestra Hall, Chicago, Prokofieff Ballet, Giulini conducting. In whatever language, I lost myself, I transcended, I sat on the edge of aesthetic experience as I had known it; I grew. My reality expanded as I lived in the movement of composer, conductor, audience, performer—all connected as a single unique thrust towards a new possibility, a new creation of an old piece of music. That interaction between myself *and* Giulini and my performing comrads and the audience enabled me to leave the notes on the page of music (on the stand in front of my eyes) and to travel past consciousness of the technical to a oneness. . . .

Civic Orchestra, an accidental community, brought to the point of being able to create community. The performance brought us face-to-face with an encounter of the unknown: ignoring the music in front of our noses and letting go, responding to Giulini's arms and body and face—to his whole being as he lived the music. But it took a mutual self-surrender. Just as each individual contributed irreplacebly to the symphonic sound, each person had to make a decision to go with the orchestra, to trust, to play. Self-discovery, reverse of power, community. But transformation could only occur at the point which was arranged and ritually expressed.

The living liturgy and the aesthetic experience give God room to move. they remove our defenses and make us vulnerable to God. And only in such experiences can god touch us; only in such moments does the kingdom of God arrive. That arrival enables us to share the Good News, not in a specific behavior or story but in a transformed way of being which affects all parts of us. Jesus did not tell people about the Kingdom of God. He lived the Kingdom, and his whole life brought people to the Kingdom through a juxtaposition of the ordinary within a startling new context. As we communicate, we are being transformed and are transforming, and indeed the Kingdom is arriving.

Communication Credo — Robert R. Miller

The source of the life-creating, energizing, animating Word—which was in the beginning and will be in the end—Yahweh Lord of Israel, Elohim Lord of all, Creator of the cosmos, Keeper of the law,

has given

the Message of reconciliation, of victory through strife, of healing and wholeness, of abundant, everlasting life; of love never ending, of justice that is sure, of swords into plowshares, of mercy free and pure,

through

the Channel of a prophet, who fortold it, a manger which contained it, a ministry which revealed it, a cross which concealed it, an empty tomb which proclaimed it

to those who have

Recieved it, who have ears to hear it, eyes to see it, hands to touch it, hearts to feel it, minds to know it, will to follow it, mouths to share it with a would in need of it.

Therefore,

we are now its ambassadors—entrusted with its Message, empowered by its Source, for the ministry of its communication.

Communication Credo — Christina Bucher

I am only human when in relationship with others. I am sister, daughter, friend, student, teacher. Though at times I need to experience my aloneness, my oneness, my always-and-ever-apartness, it is only as a self in relation to other persons that reflection upon this experience can occur.

I begin with a belief in Martin Buber's statement that "All real life is meeting." I am constantly searching for ways of opening up new relationships, just as I am continually being opened up to the possibility of newness in old relationships. Even as I am being formed by my relationships, I am a part of the forming of others.

Relationships demands reciprocity. To be in dialogue with another person, I must be willing to share of my being, to be open and authentic. Only when I open to the other person as a whole self am I able to give and to receive in relationship. The life of I-You demands that I be as much myself as I am able.

I am only human, however. Despite my hope, my intention of being an "I" to another "You," I am always being returned to the world of the object and the relationship of an "I" to an "It."

But despite the inevitability of the "I-It" relationship, I am freed and renewed by the knowledge that I am accepted in spite of imperfection. I experience the power of the Resurrection daily as I die to my old self, as I struggle with my new self, as I forgive and am forgiven.

We are called to be priests one to another. When a broken relationship occurs, inescapable as it may be, I am called to attempt to restore the relationship. Only when we are in good relationship with other persons are we in good relationship with God. And only when we are in good relationship with God can we be in a whole relationship with our brothers and sisters.

I live expectantly, in the belief in my power to create and to be created, and in the acceptance that I am human and only human.

Appendix 3

A colleague's contribution to an understanding of a theory of preaching.

The Preaching Moment: Developing and Adapting a
Communication Model Which Fits the Realities of the Present
Preaching Situation—Charles A. Wilkinson

"The preaching moment" refers to that form of communicative behavior by which an individual in a given moment presents and interprets and applies the Word of God to and for another or others. God as Word in the mind and mouth of a preacher is enough to complicate any communicative process. Added to this, the social context of the preaching moment (with all the accoutrements of religion, such as ritual, myth, magic, etc.) demands a model that can give the preacher (and hopefully the listeners) an awareness and an understanding of the complexities involved.

Communication theorists, studying the complexities of even the most simple forms of human interaction, have resorted to constructing models by which they can isolate and interrelate the functional details of the communicative process. Essentially, models are simply strategies for dealing with things terribly complex, not necessarily for the sake of solving complexities but at least for the purpose of recognizing and understanding them. If the complexities are recognized and understood, they may afford communicators motive to take more than casual care in the process. Communication models attempt to replicate the realities of the relationships and determinant factors at work in the communication process in order to at least understand the process and to improve its functioning.

In understanding a preaching model, one must realize that a great deal of theology is presumed or ignored, such as the preacher as "one commissioned by God" and the workings of grace. Since the emphasis here is communication theory and not theology, only two points will be made. First, God is not placed "outside" or "above" the people involved, but rather "within," whatever form God may take or label may be attributed. Second, God's Word is seen as creative, not as a static, sort of spoken-once-upon-a-Bible kind of thing. It is dynamic, having a present life-force particularly and peculiarity its own. While the preaching moment is more complex than the ordinary communicative situation, its model should be starkly simple. It cannot dare to presume to cover all of the variables provided by individual preachers and listeners, whatever their varying faiths, but it can and does hope to isolate the essential factors operative in any given preaching moment.

The preaching moment always involves at least two people, the preacher and the listener, each bringing to it, as the model shows, the totality of themselves. While they can never know or come to know everything about each other, they possess between them areas of identification, of shared, in-common interests which touch them into each others' lives and provide "linkage." These areas would include, most basically and for the particular moment at least, a belief in God, no matter how weakly or finely defined, no matter how different that belief may be in each. The areas would also include the shared "person-things" of each, such as humanness, in-common feelings and thinkings, and likewise shared events, proximate and remote, which the preacher and the listener have experienced or at least know about. Examples of these latter would include everything from a morning's parish liturgy, its scripture readings and hymns, to the daily newspaper and shared knowledge and awareness of what's happening in the world. It is through these that the preacher must speak to the listener. Likewise, if the listener is to respond it must be done through these areas. This is the simple Burkeian concept of *identification* which is the core of his rhetoric and the heart of this model.

Besides the areas of identification, both preacher and listener bring to the moment social-contextual influences, some of which belong to each alone, some of which they share. While it can be said that there are certain things in everyone which no other person can ever know or share, still they *are* there—and operative. The preacher has to recognize and respect the fact and presence of psychological "noise" or static or interference which every listener (and preacher) brings to the moment. A sick child at home, a shakey marriage, an impending job-change and move, and so forth. And though the preachers cannot speak through these as they can through the shared social-contextual influences (such as the building they're in, the neighborhood they're a part of, a particular parish problem they might have), they must leave room for this kind of dynamic and by some empathic-strategy let the listeners know it.

While the message of the preacher must be spoken through the areas of identification and shared interests, it should be aimed not simply at those areas but rather at the whole person, touching into the essence and substance of life. Likewise, listener response or feedback, while centered in the message and directed through those same areas, should be honest enough to touch into the essence and substance of the preacher's life. Persons preach—not ideas. Feedback, to be effective for and helpful to the preachers, must touch honestly into themselves. While this basic model sits flat upon the page, the dimensional dynamic of Dance's helical model is presumed to be operative. Both preacher and listener evolve out of God's creative Word. The preaching moment should be an essential part of the phenomenon, with both preacher and listener sharing in the life-force of God's Word.

While all that has been said about the preacher-listener relationship described in Figure 1 applies here, it must also be said that the preacher must not lump together all of the listeners into one category or stereotype. Each brings to the moment, as Figure 2 tries to demonstrate, an identity, an individuality (L1, 2, 3, 4) which the preacher must recognize and respect. As the preachers speak, they should aim to establish dyadic communication between themselves and the individual listeners. Obviously, the larger the audience, the more difficult this becomes. On a person-to-person, one-to-one basis, the areas of identification are more easily discovered and more workable, depending upon the knowledge each has of each. On a one-to-many basis, however, these areas necessarily thin out so that the preacher has to establish identification most times in terms of their own shared humanness, or which is more frequently the case, of some in-common concept of God.

Regarding the social-contextual influences, complications are also multiplied and once again the preacher's task is made more difficult. However, the opportunities for feedback-response are more increased, even though because of the number of listeners involved it would seem that such a possibility would be rendered more remote. This might be explained by the audience's tendency to see itself as a singular phenomenon rather than as a phenomenon made up of singular people. That is, while it is the preacher's responsibility to respect and address the individualities of one's listeners, they in turn may not respect their own and lose themselves safely "in the crowd." By the same token, the listeners have the responsibility of respecting the

Figure 1.

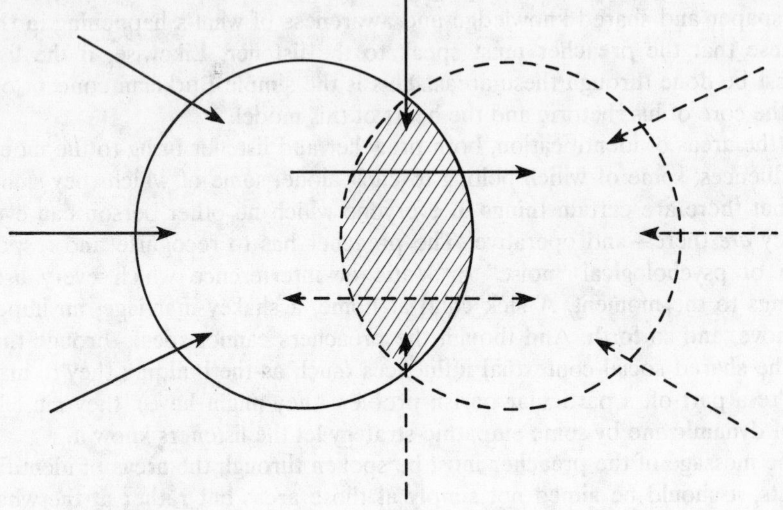

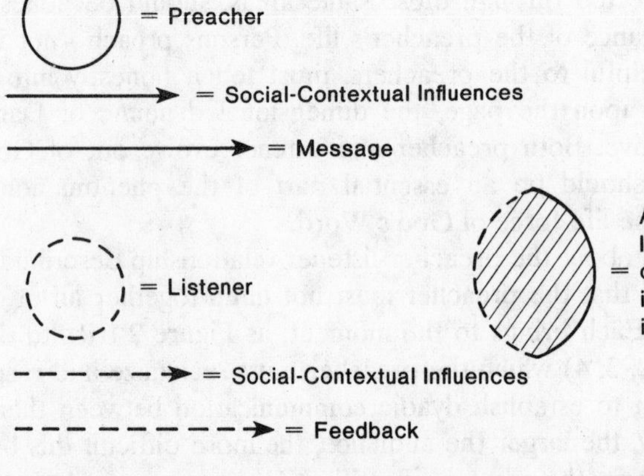
= Preacher
= Social-Contextual Influences
= Message
= Listener
Area of Identification: = of shared, in-common interests
= Social-Contextual Influences
= Feedback

preacher's individuality and not lumping the preacher together with whatever stereotypes that might bias them.

One can begin to see in Figure 2 many of the complexities of the preaching moment, if only in terms of the preacher-listener relationship. However, nothing has been said about the listener-listener relationships operative in any group, the communicative behaviors among them which is another complexity that, although not falling within the limits of this work, the model adequately describes and is, therefore, another factor which the aware preacher must consider.

If all that has been said thus far is true, it seems that the preacher's key strategy has to be identification. Perhaps the "seeming" art of this will dissolve if one can answer the question: what happens if the preacher fails to establish and speak through these areas of identification? Figures 3 and 4 provide a visual answer and illustrate a distortion phenomenon that might be called "swallowing."

Figure 2.

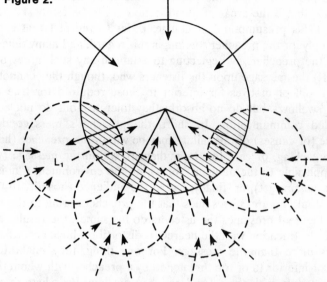

Figure 3.

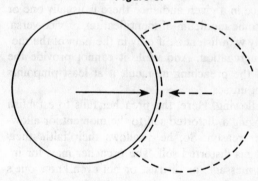

Figure 4.

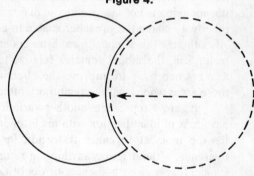

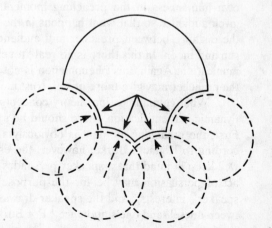

Both figures presume that in the preaching moment, the preacher is the dominant and determinative force, that if the areas of identification are to be established at all, it will be the preacher's doing. (This presumption, of course, cedes to the fact that at times the listeners themselves can supply for the preacher's failing in this regard, and many times do.)

In Figure 3 the preacher, by neglecting to establish any such areas of identification, intrudes (force feeds) the message upon the listeners who, though they cannot or will not understand it, receive it out of motives far inferior to those required for true and effective communication. They swallow—but do no absorb; they tolerate—but do not actually share in the preacher's intended communication. In short, the preacher's message does not reach the hearers. The cause (or causes) of this failure may be within the preacher (having less than adequate talent for preaching, or care for the audience), within the message (vagueness, "above" the audience, inapplicable to the moment), or within the environment ("noise," a malfunctioning microphone, a passing jet), or, finally, within the audience (hostility to the message, a personal alienation). While Figure 3 presumes that the preachers bring to the moment the totality of themselves (as Figure 4 presumes the listeners do the same), the result of their failure to establish any sort of identification with the hearers is distortion which, according to this model, effects the listeners more than the message. For one thing, they might feel left out of the preacher's world, or inferior to or too threatened by a preacher with whom they cannot identify, or who does not identify with them. And so, they swallow, for whatever motives. And since something less than true communication is happening, a resigned alienation, at least for the moment, is usually the result so that neither message nor feedback can get through. Obviously this phenomenon is not as absolute as diagrammed since in a given audience there is usually one or other with whom the preacher is able to establish some modicum of identification, or vice-versa. Also, though this is not shown, listeners can identify with listeners, if only in the pain of the moment. Still, the model remains relative to any congregation. And while it cannot provide the answers necessary to improve the effectiveness of the preaching moment, it at least pinpoints those areas where that moment more often than not misses.

Figure 4 represents another variation of swallowing. Here, the preacher fails to establish any areas of identification with his listeners by bringing a distorted self to the moment, or allowing the moment to cause distortion for whatever reason. So, he swallows their faith, their tolerance, without giving anything in return except his distorted self. The preacher may, for instance, fear a given audience, or doubt one's own message, or distrust or not even know one's own humanness in the preaching moment. The preacher may set personal safety "above" a given audience so that what happens in the moment is closer to eclipse than to sharing. Indeed, the distance between preacher and audience is too often comparable to the distance between sun and moon. In this there is no real "touching into" each other's life, no linkage, no true communication. Again, this phenomenon is not as absolute as diagrammed, for in a given audience the preacher may give more of self, trust more of self, to one listener than to another.

What communication theory concepts are operative in the model as given? Since its core dynamic is identification, more should be said about what that means and how it is established. First, the preaching moment is obviously a rhetorical moment. It is essentially persuasive. According to Kenneth Burke, however, the essence of persuasion is identification. "We might as well keep in mind that a speaker persuades an audience by the use of stylistic identificatons; his act of persuasion may be for the purpose of causing the audience to identify itself with the speaker's interests," and the speaker draws on identification of interests to establish rapport between oneself and one's audience.[1] For Burke, identification means that things or people, different in other ways, may have one common factor in which they are consubstantial or substantially the same . . . In this Burkeian sense, people identify themselves with causes, religions, movements, with heroic types in the movies, with classes or types of people who buy any given make of motorcar, or live in one or another neighborhood. Identification . . . is a belonging to a group of people or a becoming one with them through at least some one formality of common purpose or ideal . . . Identification . . . is consubstantiality, belonging. It means the same as persuasion because it covers all that persuasion covers, and yet it goes beyond persuasion in covering the whole field of motivational language, conscious and unconscious, in the rhetoric of conformity and appeal.[2]

Burke sees identification occurring in interests or in principles, even in motives, but at no time does that obliterate their uniqueness:

> A is not identical with his colleague, B. But insofar as their interests are joined, A is identified with B. Or he may identify himself with B even when their interests are not joined, if he assumes that they are, or is persuaded to believe so . . . In being identified with B, A is "substantially one" with a person other than himself. Yet, at the same time he remains unique, an individual locus of motives . . . two persons may be identified in terms of some principle they share in common, an "identification" that does not deny their distinctness.[3]

Thus, the main task of the preacher, if one is to persuade, must be to establish identification, to become "consubstantial" with the listeners. The "old rhetorics" would call this "audience analysis" but it is and involves something far deeper, which begins not with the audience but with the preacher. How can this happen? First, the preachers must honestly face themselves and ask what part is "faith." Just that, no more. Yet, there is far more to the preaching moment than just that. There are people interacting, feelings intermingling, human individualities being shared. Yet, too many times the people are lost, the feelings ignored or denied, and the human individualities "gotten out of the way." Faith as an identification strategy is as untranslatable as the concept itself. It is too many times a vague and "pretty" thing, something that can keep both preacher and listener conveniently away from the realities of themselves and their worlds. Not that it can't effect "linkage." Rather, in the preaching moment faith should be the first dynamic to be *presumed,* not to be used. People and feelings and human individualities can provide a far more tangible "touching into" one anothers' lives and can add to a presumed faith a not-too-often-presumed understanding or strength.

Secondly, the preacher must consider the listeners, asking, what part of themselves they share. Again, too often preachers speak through scripture and not through people, knowing and recognizing them and understanding them well enough to discover new and effective ways for them to hear the Word of God. Alfonso M. Nebreda, S. J. in his *Kerygma in Crisis,* sums up these first two points;

> Our (preachers') job is to convey a message—and a message is essentially from someone to someone. A message means communication, conveying something meaningful. It follows that the preacher must, in truth, be the first believer. His belief, and his desire to share it with others, moves him to go out of himself, to sacrifice his own preferences, in order to see through the other's eyes and feel through the other's heart. His first goal is to establish a real human dialogue. This means he must take the other seriously.[4]

Identification can also be established not only through the people involved but also through the social context of the situation.

> The process of human communication cannot be explained apart from social context. Communication does not occur in a sociocultural vacuum; it is not a "pure" process, without context or background. Every social situation forms a pattern, a context, that governs the ongoing flow and effects interpersonal

behavior. In the literature on communication theory, the notion of social context refers to forces influencing communication in an immediate, specific setting, and to those forces that govern the flow if information and patterns of influence from reference group to reference group.[5]

Again, what is too often ignored, for whatever reasons, in the preaching moment is the simple factor of situation. In it exist "forces" that can not only "influence communication" but also create new processes, new means or media which can establish external identification as well as internal. For example, in the shared areas of social context indicated in the model, a preacher can create within the church or parish an atmosphere that can eliminate the vertical stereotype that usually distances preacher from listeners, or even listeners from listeners. Or by admitting the presence of unshared areas, preachers can at least make themselves and their listeners aware of these influences. Patterns long established can be questioned, evaluated, and perhaps rejected for new ways of saying what really can't be added to. An awareness of the complexities of the moment, on the part of both preacher and listeners, can help to establish an unspoken identification that might be called respect. And even though, as Wayne E. Brockreide states, "The substance of a rhetorical act is rarely located in the situation: it more characteristically focuses on the interpersonal and attitudinal categories," still, many if not all of the accidentals of social context can certainly clarify and steady the characteristic focus of rhetoric and likewise of the preaching moment. To ignore these is to risk blurriness that confuses more than teaches or persuades.

But even a knowledge of self, of audience, of situation isn't always sufficient for effective communication, or for full use of the preaching moment. An unspoken premise here, inherent and essential to the given model, is this: *communication is not just SAYING something; it's having it HEARD.* To achieve this in our culture or society demands something more than the patterned, purely verbal ways of preaching, if only because of our "occupational numbness" due to the media explosion. According to Shannon and Weaver, while predictability in mathematics is something to be desired, in communication it is equatd with redundancy and can thus have a negative effect on the communicative process. People do not listen well (if at all) when they sense that they have already heard something. Therefore, Shannon and Weaver speak of the need for *entropy* in communication. For them entropy is simply randomness, or lack of predictability. Its presence can heighten or intensify the communicative moment if only because people listen differently, more intently according to the level of unpredictability. So that, in the preaching moment, new and creative means of expressing the Word of God, unpatterned ways of preaching, unpulpited and unvested, the use of vocabularies that reflect "being" as well as Bible, dialogical experiences, and so forth, can allow the preacher and listener alike a freedom to identify, to share, to truly communicate, to hear in ways unheard before. However, even more than entropy is required. It must also be creative. The off-handed randomness of babbling or of "being casual or 'real'" or of responding to the moment can at times produce effective communication. But those times are too rare for any preacher to risk the presumption of attaining spontaneous spiritual combustion. This creativity includes all that has been said above, and has to be consistent with the moment as well as with all of the elements involved. A suddenly slammed door is entropic but it doesn't necessarily communicate an intended message. Creative entropy must center on the preacher's intended message, not for the sake of creatively saying it but for the far more complex purpose of having it heard . . . and understood . . . and responded to. Henri Nouwen, in his *Creative Ministry,* stresses this point most clearly in his excellent chapter on "Creative Preaching," subtitled, "Beyond the Retelling of the Story."[6]

Two additional factors involved in the process of identification yet to be considered are noise and feedback. "Noise in its simplest form is the addition or omission of a symbol in the communicative chain which results in a discrepancy between the message transmitted and the message received (or in more human terms, the message intended and the message perceived)."[7] While this is a mechanical definition, it can also apply to the psychological processes involved in the preaching moment, that is, it can be internal as well as external. Noise can be present within a person as well as within a situation, an environment. Unless preachers are aware of the workings of such a phenomenon they might find it almost impossible to establish workable identifications with the listeners. And while noise can be entropic in the communicative process, entropy, if it is sufficiently creative, can utilize noise to heighten the communicative moment.

Feedback can be descriptively defined as a listener's response to a speaker's message that can be perceived by the speaker to answer the question, "How am I communicating?" It can be as simple as listening to one's own voice or to the verbal responses of others, or as sophisticated as reading the non-verbal expressions and responses of an audience—such as a smile, a nod of the head, a fidgeting or restlessness, and so forth. Since listeners can easily mask their real reactions to messages, and since different cultures have different ways of communicating social approval or disapproval, a speaker must not only make an effort to be aware of feedback but also know how to interpret it. In the preaching moment, verbal feedback has been a rare phenomenon, at least till recent years, if only because of the vertical, "up there with God" stance too often and too easily assumed by the preacher. Also, because of this "distancing" of the preacher, non-verbal response was generally gone unread. As a result, a valuable source of motivation, whether in terms of encouragement or suggestions for improvement, has been left untapped, as well as a source for discovering further areas of identification.

There are many more concepts in communication theory pertinent to the model given here. Heider's concept of balance,[8] Osgood and Tannebaum's principle of congruity,[9] Festinger's theory of cognitive dissonance,[10] attitudes, ethos, interpersonal network, can all find their place within the given model. The complexities of human interaction will never be solved or explained by any one communication model, or any number of them. Nor will the model given here solve the complexities of the preaching moment. Its modest hope is to bring to preachers a visual understanding of some of the dynamics which current communication theory has defined for other communicative situations; or if not an understanding, then at least an excuse (or reason) for constructing other models that will help to make the preaching moment all that it is meant to be—an experience in true communication between God and people.

Notes:

1. Kenneth Burke, *A Grammar of Motives and a Rhetoric of Motives* (Cleveland, 1962) p. 57.
2. Daniel Fogarty, S. J., *Roots for a New Rhetoric* (New York, 1959), pp. 74–76.
3. Alfonso M. Nebreda, S. J., *Kerygma in Crisis* (Chicago, 1965) p. 104.
4. Kenneth Burke, pp. 545–546.

5. Kenneth K. Sereno and C. David Mortensen, eds., *Foundations of Communication Theory* (New Hork, 1970), p. 292.
6. Henri J. M. Nouwen, *Creative Ministry* (New York, 1971) pp. 21–40.
7. Allan R. Broadhurst and Donald K. Darnell, "An Introduction to Cybernetics and Information Theory," in Sereno and Mortensen, p. 70.
8. F. Heider, "Attitudes and Cognitive Organization," *Journal of Psychology,* vol. 21, 1946, pp. 107–112.
9. C. E. Osgood and P. H. Tannebaum, "The Principle of Congruity in the Prediction of Attitude Change," *Psychology Review,* vol. 62, 1955, pp. 42–55.
10. Leon Festinger, *A Theory of Cognitive Dissonance* (Evanston, Illinois, 1957); Additional theory consideration can be found in Frank E. X. Dance's *Human Communication Theory* (New York, 1967) and Claude E. Shannon and Warren Weaver's *The Mathematical Theory of Communication* (Urbana, Illinois, 1949).

Appendix 4

Skills involved in the art of reading Scripture aloud also applicable to the art of preaching as shared story.

Bible Reading—A Communication Act

The Bible when read aloud moves us to hear its message more clearly than when read silently.

"Write on the newsprint the changes you would like most in your worship services." Two groups listed as their number one that the Bible be read aloud more meaningfully. That is no surprise if, indeed, the Bible is our mainstay as Christians and our main staple as worshippers. The Bible is a junction where God and God's people meet.

But why number one? Are we so unfamiliar that we already know the meaning before it is read? ("Oh, that's the story of the good Samaritan; I already know that one.") Or are we like the poets who read their own material with little expression because as readers they already know? Is it because we think the Bible was written for the eye and not for the ear?

Is oral reading so badly done because we fail to sense or believe its revolutionary message? Or is it because we do not know how to use the tools to release its message when it is read aloud? One teacher of oral interpretation tells the class, "If it is not well expressed, either you don't understand it, or else you do not know how to release it."

Assuming that as a result of Bible study we know the meaning, let us concentrate on tools for releasing its meaning. We need not become like performer William Booth who gives the entire book of Mark in one program, with few props and little makeup, whose memorized words neither sound memorized nor read. He recreates the entire book, one time suggesting how Jesus thought and felt, then the Sadducees or Pharisees, then the narrator. All the time he remains William Booth, yet we have come to know how each and all feel and think. Booth is not acting, but reading.

The Reader's Comprehension

How well does the reader understand the meaning of the materials? Listeners should not have to do all the work. The reader should know the answers to the following questions: What is the passage's theme? What is the order of thoughts and feelings that are part of the theme? the climax? the mood? the imagery? the spirit and spiritual overtone? An outline to aid understanding includes theme, sequence of thought and feeling, climax, mood, and imagery. These answers could be written down. It is well worth the time to figure out the place of thought and

From the Bible in Worship by LeRoy Kennel, published by Faith and Life Press and Mennonite Publishing House, published 1987.

feeling in literature. If one is to help others to enjoy or to worship with the Bible, readers must also know and enjoy it.

One helpful grid for analysis is to look for logical and emotional settings and logical and emotional details. Four squares can be drawn with answers placed inside.[1]

	SETTING	DETAILS
L O G I C A L	*Author's theme* Author's method of presenting theme (description, exposition, narration, characterization, dialog, and poetics)	*Meanings of words and phrases* Word relations in sentences
E M O T I O N A L	Author's character and philosophy Author's mood and motivation	Relations of meanings to imagery; various kinds of images (visual, of sight, motor, of movement; auditory, of sounds; tactile, of touch; olfactory, of smell; gustatory, of taste; thermic, of temperature)

LOGICAL EMOTION

Comprehension comes with a sense of the Bible's worth. Bible reading is a privilege. In a public reading, one represents both God, the original writer(s), and the congregation, as well as oneself. Therefore, the reader cannot take reading of the Bible lightly. Bible reading is both an act of worship in which one lifts up Bible reading as one's own offering.

The goal should not be to get congratulations on how well one reads or even to think of asking, "How am I doing?" It is rather, "How are they doing?" "The joy is to hear the people say how much more they understood and felt the Scripture. Checking one's attitude from time to time can help cultivate the purpose of oral interpretation: the re-creation of the printed page for the benefit of others. This requires sensitivity to a congregation. How are they responding to the word? How as readers can we quicken and deepen their appreciation? Thus, the reader listens to the hearers, asking what can improve reading as a means of listening.

After the thought and mood have been grasped as a whole (and as parts), the reader needs to do groupings or phrasings. Although natural groups include pargraphs and sentences, word-grouping or phrasing here refer to shorter divisions called breath-groups or phrases. The phrases themselves are grammatical groupings for the ear, not for the eye. Having grasped the thought, the reader divides it for ear thoughts—regardless of eye punctuation.

[1]Charles H. Woolbert and Severina E. Nelson, The Art of Interpretative Speech (Appleton-Century-Crofts, Inc., 1945).

How many words equal an ear-thought? That depends upon the size and character of the audience, the purpose of the reader, and the difficulty or strangeness of the thought. Groupings followed by pauses indicate that a given speech idea is finished. It is also a time to briefly look back, point forward, or just savor what has been said.

Eye punctuation (such as commas, designed to assist the mind in getting the message) are not the same for the ear. If a sibling says that the English teacher gave an "F" on punctuation, reply, "Ah, forget it, and all punctuations unless they help one to undersand what you're sharing." So with ear punctuations. Forget ear punctuations, too, unless they help one to understand what is shared.

A new set of punctuations, however, is needed for giving via the ear. The point is that phrasing is determined by an ear (speech) thought and not by an eye (written) thought. Using a slash (/) to mark pauses between speech thoughts, this occasion (the pause following the speech thought) is also the time to breathe, although it should not be necessary to do so at every pause. In the sample below, the breathing times are arbitrarily suggested with an asterisk (*).

> The necessary art of punctuation/cannot be relied upon /as a satisfactory guide for vocal phrasing. */Although it sometimes happens that pauses coincide with punctuation marks, /no definite generalizations can be made. */Punctuations help to indicate the structure of the sentence to the eye and to the mind. /Vocal phrasing,/on the other hand, */allows the meaning of the sentence/to become clear to the mind/through the ear. */There are times when the punctuation mark is slighted /as a guide to phrasing, */and at other times/ phrasing is necessary /even though the writer has found no need for punctuation whatsoever./

As can be seen above, breaks or pauses occur between subjects and verbs. That is permissible and practiced, even though a writer would seldom do that for a reader's eye.

The slight or longer pause is determined by one's comprehension. In Jesus' statement, "Drink ye all of it" (Matt. 26:27, KJV), should the diagonal line (pause) be placed after *ye* or after *all?* These are two different thoughts. If one decides that it be after *all,* it is good theology to recognize that we should not pick and choose what parts of Christ we will drink. If that were the message of the day, what would be wrong for the communion celebrant to say, "Drink ye/*all* of it." Playing it safe may lead the celebrant to say also that everyone should hear the challenge, "Drink ye *all*/of it."

Who hasn't chuckled when the Christmas Eve reader paused after *babe?* "And they came in haste, and found Mary, and Joseph, and the babe/lying in a manger" (Luke 2:16, KJV). Maybe they were all in the manger—Hollywood sets do not have the last word.

Comprehension requires that one word within a given phrase receive stress. It carries most of the thought-load, and thus, it is the spotlighted idea or feeling. That accepted word is set apart from other words (just as in a word with more than one syllable, more than one vowel, one sound is stressed to distinguish it from the other syllables). So, if in the opening phrase of Psalm 23, "The Lord is my shepherd," one desires to say, it is not the president nor the premier who's calling the shots in my life but the Other One, then one particular word is mentally (and physically) underlined: "The *Lord* is my shepherd."

If, however, one wants to stress present tense, not talking about last week's experience, or even two years ago, then the next words gets the spotlight, "The Lord *is* my shepherd." If one is under conviction to give a personal testimony, to speak for oneself rather than for one's mother, brother, or neighbor, then stress the third word, "The Lord is *my* shepherd."

And if one wishes to witness the truth that God is not a Kleenex, that God is not merely someone to whom you tip a hat, that God is not merely someone who pushes one to the next filling station when one has run out of gas, that God is not that all important credit card, but God is rather an advocate attorney who is there to counsel in life and death matters, to guide and assist in management (and for good reasons, since God owns it all in the first place, and because we've invited God to do so in the second place), then read, "The Lord is my *shepherd.*"

What if you say, "I want all four meanings; they're all good ones, all true?" Sorry, then you need four different readers or four different occasions. Reading the Bible aloud is selective business. If each word were spotlighted in the same reading, it would be as meaningless as to not call out any particular meaning within the phrase. It would be a bit more humorous to call out each one, whereas to call out none is sad. As it might be written, "Choose you this day, which word you shall stress."

The Reader's Assimilation

Reading the Bible aloud has a second *shun* that should not be shunned—assimilation. This effort in Bible reading "makes it one's own." Comprehension is the student role; assimilation, the servant role, where one gives oneself entirely to the text's meaning. Empathy, appropriation, abandonment, appreciation, and paraphrase are emphasized—and visualization. While reading Psalm 23, one sees the shepherd image. Visualizing produces an appropriate emotional reaction which in turn helps the voice reflect the text's meaning. At the same time, it is "the word becoming flesh." Something new is added, "the gospel according to you." The reader becomes a prism, that piece of glass which held to the white light reflects different colors on the wall. If Psalm 23 is read by five different readers, and if all emphasize the same word in a given thought-unit, five different readings still result, because there are five respective assimilations via visualization.

How do we visualize? (1) Picture what David meant by Psalm 23. (2) Call to mind the image of something that you have seen, a past memory of a shepherd out on the western plains herding sheep. (3) Recall instances of despair banished by faith after seeing Jesus Christ as a caring shepherd.

Paraphrase is a recommended way to assimilate biblical material. Whereas comprehension permits a précis (a one-sentence summary in one's own word, i.e., David is convinced that God will see him through this battle), a paraphrase pushes one to restate that one sentence (a *then* meaning) into a longer *now* meaning, i.e., "If I lose my job . . . if the enemy attacks . . . if I lose my family or friends . . . get cancer . . . I will still have security—my best friend." Assimilation puts biblical material into one's own words as a result of puting oneself into the situation made by the author. Even if one's only audience is oneself, it is a mini-act of worship.

One's own paraphrase can be supplemented by other's paraphrases. Personal favorites include Leslie Brant's psalms, Clarence Jordan's parables, B. D. Napier's biblical history, J. B. Phillips' epistles, and Peter Ediger's prophetic reports on North America.

Honesty characterizes Scripture reading. Visualization and paraphrase do not need to be nice, safe, or pretty. If you are angry with your brother or sister, and you read that "thou shalt not kill," get in touch with the time when you killed the mosquito that was buzzing around while you were trying to sleep. When reading the story of the good Samaritan, get in touch with the beaten one's plight. If you cannot recall someone else's pain, consider your own. (I might remember when after returning late from a Gospel Team trip at Hesston College, I reached into my briefcase only to find that I had placed my safety razor there, and it had come apart, and now the blade was stuck in my middle finger—over two thirds of an inch. A scar still remains.) If you read aloud, "take no thought for tomorrow," you can get in touch by saying to yourself, "Yes, but you don't have to can peaches for ten kids." Or, "That's all right for the rich."

Assimilation skill is a matter of practice. When done consciously and when monitored, reviewed, and replayed (on the tape recorder), do it once again—this time doing just what comes naturally. Assimilation makes the material seem like your own. You speak the Bible's words as your own. It happens best when after understanding the selection (the thought and feeling of the words, the purpose and intent of the author) you see or imagine it, then paraphrase it into your own experiences.

The Reader's Communication

How does one express one's thoughts and feelings with one's congregation? Having obtained an impression of the printed page, having made the material one's own, then one shares it with others. The skills are the same whether one's congregation is one, ten, one hundred, one thousand. Three channels are possible for sending our messages. If one chooses to use only one, one forfeits stereo.

Vocal Expression
"Are you an Ephraimite?"
"No."
"Then say Shibboleth."
"Sibboleth."
When this pronunciation quiz was administered by a Gileadite who caught a suspected Ephraimite trying to cross the River Jordan, the purpose was to see whether the suspect was telling the truth (Judg. 12:5–6). The prisoner may vow, of course, that he was a Gileadite but his speech would give him away. Gileadites called an ear of corn "shibboleth," not "sibboleth." An error of one consonant would cost one's life, hardly consonant with the value of life. Nevertheless, it was a fatal error.

Harsh penalties are placed on poor communication. Japanese who claimed to be Chinese or Filipino during World War II were asked by American captors to say "Lalapalooza." Because the Japanese do not "hear" L sounds, the prisoner might have said "raraparooza." Once upon a time a young lady hearing Peter speak, declared that he was a Galilean, a follower of Jesus. Poor Peter: he denied it (as if one's speech could be denied).

Vocal effectiveness puts the elements of speech to good use just as a good carpenter must know how to handle wood-working tools. Another analogy—music instruments need to be in good shape, as well as orchestrated by a vocal carpenter/conductor: pitch, rate, volume, quality, and pronunciation. Each must be adequate. When each is also *varied,* the instruments total ten.

Pitch is one of the elements of voice. It has to do with highness and lowness of sound. It results from the type of emotional reaction one has. Our reactions cause bodily tensions which make different voice responses. Sometimes he has monopitch or monopatterns, and also tones poorly supported by breath. But we can be expressive: If the car is hit by a careless driver, one's pitch sounds higher and tense. Pitch portrays the Scripture's mood. And it should be supported with breath (controlled exhalation). Otherwise, our high becomes shrill and our low pitch monotonous. After one has established one's optimum pitch level (usually about one-third from the bottom of one's total pitch range), it is important that there also be variation. Varying pitch can be achieved by steps (movements up or down) and by slides within a word. These changes are differences of pitch between or within a word.

Time, a second tool, is the fastness or slowness of utterance, as well as the holding of the stressed syllable or key word in the grouping. Bad grouping and jerkiness are usually caused by poor timing. Normally, one can rely on the meaning and moon expressed by the author to determine tempo or rate. Expression for others of that meaning and mood can be best attained if there be variation on the key word by the method of prolonging the vowel, by "pulling taffy."

Volume is determining vocal effectiveness; it is one's loudness or softness. Volume is controlled by three sets of muscles located in the shoulders, ribs, and diaphragm-abdomen. The last mentioned set provides the best control of breathing, and serves as a governor on a car to give both the needed fuel to operate the speech motor (the vibration of the vocal folds in the larynx) as well as to conserve the fuel use. The throat should remain relaxed. The pressure is from below not from around the throat. Otherwise, loudness tends to result in harshness and lowness tends to result in breathiness. Apply force to vary the volume according to the sense of the thought. Again, adequacy must be altered with variation.

Vocal quality also determines vocal effectiveness. The quality of the voice is dependent upon physical makeup and the amplification of tone. Bad voice qualities include nasality, denasality, breathiness, harshness, hoarseness, and thinness. These problems can be minimized. Threre are two chief ways to improve voice quality. All three resonating chambers need to be appropriately opened and relaxed. The first area where the vibrating sound enters is the pharynx (throat). It ought to be opened up the size of a large bologna rather than that of a small wiener. The effect is much that of a yawn. The throat needs to hang loose like draperies rather than tense like a metal wall.

The oral cavitiy, better known as the mouth, also needs to be open. One should not worry about gold fillings being stolen or a poor dental profile being seen. What calls attention to itself is a voice quality resulting from a closed mouth, in which sound does not have opportunity to resonate. Certain vowels grow best in the respective areas of the mouth: back, middle, and front.

The third resonating chamber, the nose, is used only in the English language for the m, n, and ng sounds. For all other English sounds, the uvula at the back of the soft palate has to provide a trap door so sound does not enter up there and produce nasality. Stopping a moment to listen, one soon discovers how many lazy soft palates there are. A starting exercise for quality improvement is to consciously try for a maximum of echo with the least effort. Adequacy is a criterion, but so is variation.

The fifth (and tenth) tool is *articulation*—the shaping of resonators to produce vowels, diphthongs, and consonants. Vowels consist of relatively musical tones, whereas consonants are a noise produced through friction of stoppage of air. Diphthongs are a combination of vowel sounds produced as one sound. The English language is difficult when it comes to matching up the eye and ear alphabet: there are over forty sounds and only twenty-six letters.

Faulty articulation may be due also to organic causes. A frequent problem is the omission of sounds, adding of others, distorting the rate or extreme variations. The two major tools of articulation for expressing the Bible can be slightly renamed: adequacy becomes *exactness* and variation becomes *naturalness*. After one has achieved precise emitting of the sounds, one does not want a "schoolmarm's diction" in which everything is said so evenly and clearly that it is no longer natural. So, we let some things transpose a bit. Instead of saying all the sounds in handkerchief we omit the d. Many times, the a will be so unstressed that it is a mere quick and almost quiet uh. Naturalness is especially important in reading Scripture, for what Scripture points to, worship in truth, has little time for affection.

Let's apply some of these vocal tools to a given Scripture (like Psalm 23:1a). Assuming that our idea is that Yahweh God is our chief sponsor rather than the president or premier, *Lord* is underlined and stressed by rate prolonging (holding the vowel). The effect could be described as letting up on the accelerator of the car at that point, just because the mental traffic is heavy there, and not because a traffic officer is present. We don't drive at the same speed all the time: we slow when there's something particular to watch.

But rate changing only is not enough to properly call attention to *Lord*. Holding the vowel only will make the word *Lord* sound boring. If it is prolonged with pitch change, too, especially if it is a double inflection (the sound wave looks like the teeth of a saw), the word *Lord* is both interesting and communicative. One can also call upon a third tool of volume. But *Lord* won't be shouted, although a good number of readers of the Bible do just that on their key words. To use just a bit of more volume on the queen word makes the meaning go a longer way. Another possibility is to use a bit less volume. The point: variation highlights *Lord*. One can also use a pitch of voice quality change to imply reverence. All of these tools must be employed for maximum expression if perchance one's thought and feeling is *is* or *my* or *shepherd*.

A playful summary of vocal expression of a biblical passage is "Get the sense out of there and give it to us!" Some applied rules include: 1) Assume a "you are there" attitude; 2) Take your cues from literary clues; 3) Use a sit-down tone in a stand-up position; 4) Put direct discourse into vocal quotation marks; 5) Fuse thought (phrasing) and feeling (weak and strong vowels).

For an exercise other than Psalm 23:1a, one can practice on any sentence; for example, "I didn't tell John you were stupid." One can express this in seven different ways. (1) Someone else had it. (2) I'm keeping the fact a secret. (3) I only hinted at it. (4) I told everyone but John. (5) I said that someone around here was stupid. (6) I told him you still are stupid. (7) I only voiced my conviction that you weren't very smart.[2]

Visual expression

Visual cues confirm and complete the vocal ones or cancel them. Positively, we have another way of saying it. Specific tools include: eyes, face, body, walk, posture, gesture, dress. Who cannot tell by just looking at someone if there be sadness, surprise, or satisfaction, or whether there be admiration, affection, anxiety, or anger? Whatever one does it ought to be consistent with what one says, and so that our yea be yea and our nay be nay. What we do viually ought to reinforce what people her. (Although most research now says that the visual is the primary message with the vocal being the reinforcer.) When one reads the Bible, one's body ought to take a secondary and even minimum role. The body's high calling is to suggest the

[2]Several resources for supplementing the exercises listed here, as well as for visual and verbal expression, include: Harold A. Brack, Effective Oral Interpretation for Religious Leaders (Prentice Hall, 1964); Charlotte I. Lee, Oral Reading of the Scriptures (Houghton Mifflin, 1974); Dwight E. Stevenson and Charles F. Diehl, Reaching People from the Pulpit (Harper,1958).

meaning. One does not become Jesus as an actor would, but one must allow the muscles to em-
pathically feel as Jesus feels when he says, "Get behind me, Satan" or "Neither do I condemn
you."

The eyes do not always have it. When one looks down at the text, the eyes can be taught
to see a grouping followed by that pnciled in diagonal line (and even possibly a second grouping). Assuming that we have done some previous thinking about the text, one's eyes can now lift
toward the congregation. During that lifting, a lot of good things can happen. The mind
refamiliarizes, revisualizes. Just as a cellist who practiced so well last week and yesterday has to
relive it in the playing this afternoon before the actual audience, even so the reader needs to
also relive the phrase—right now. Keeping the eyes on the congregation, the one grouping, and
possibly two, are shared, with the eyes staying with the congregation to the very last sound
before dropping to find the next thoughts. The eyes when listed to the congregation do not go
back and forth like a water oscillating sprinkler, but staying with one flower (person) here and
then another one there, and then possibly swooping or scooping a bunch. Not always will there
bea meeting of the eyes since some material is reflective or like a soliloquy. When a congregation is eavesdropping, it's permissible to let the eyes focus just above the heads of the congregation. Normally, however, your "angel-olatry" will not be that of the guardian angels located
"way down there" (in hell) or "way up there" (in heaven) or just outside the windows (flying by
and waving at one). The angels are right in the room with you, the people of the congregation
who are waiting to have that eyeball-to-eyeball experience on the intention of the Scripture.

One's muscular responses will be imitated by a congregation, just as surely as the young
piano student's parents go through some of the same grimaces at the recital. Of course, they
feel the pain of missed notes but also they have the exuberance of right ones. Perchance the
pianist child sees this in turn, his failure or success keeps building. A communicating reader
knows that success breeds success and visual communication breeds visual communication.

Whatever the visual tool be, it should not call attention to itself. It is a servant of the
Lord. Modest dress and jewelry are presumed.

Verbal expression

Many, if not all, Scriptures need introductions. One rarely starts reading the newspaper
out loud at a kitchen table but one may say, "Hey, do you remember when . . . well, this com-
mentator surely has a strange idea of what happened." So why wouldn't one also say, "She really didn't know how to say thank you to Jesus. No one had ever treated her this way before. She
glanced around the room and saw her perfumes. She knew then how to say it." Then the Scripture could be read. Functional introductions cause a listener to think, "Hmmm, I believe I
would like to tune in for this one." Transitions, inferences, and adaptations to audience needs,
capacities, and time limits are the guidelines for verbal expressions that make a difference.